Baltimore Beauties and Beyond

C&T PUBLISHING

Baltimore Beauties
and Beyond
Studies in
Classic Album Quilt Appliqué
Volume One

by Elly Sienkiewicz

Title Page Calligraphy by Walter J. Filling

Front Cover Photo:
Silhouette Wreath: Block design and appliqué by Elly Sienkiewicz.
Pattern # 16, block A-2 from quilt #7
"The Fascinating Ladies of Bygone Baltimore"
Quilting: Designed and quilted by Hazel B. Reed Ferrell
Photo: Sharon Risedorph

Copyright © 1989 Eleanor Patton Hamilton Sienkiewicz

Photography by Garrison Studios, Sharon Risedorph, Donald Sienkiewicz, Stan Sienkiewicz,
Sotheby's Photography Studio, Greg Staley, and Steve Tuttle.

Edited by Sayre Van Young
Berkeley, California

Illustrations by Lisa Krieshok
Berkeley, California

Design/Production Coordination by Bobbi Sloan Design
Berkeley, California

Desktop Published by Nancy McClure
Kensington, California

Display Typography by The Graphics Connection
Oakland, California

Published by C&T Publishing
P.O. Box 1456
Lafayette, California 94549

ISBN: 0-914881-23-x

Library of Congress Card No: 89-060479

First Edition

10 9 8

Printed in China

Contents

The Color Section follows page 80.

Acknowledgments

Thank you to the quiltmakers with whom I've been in classes and who have shared so much, and especially to those needleartists whose work either graces these pages or waits in the wings for Volumes II and III; to Carolie and Tom Hensley for their faith in this book; and to the magazine publishers, convention entrepreneurs, shop owners, and guilds who enable me to work with the quilting I love.

Thank you to the supportive staff of this book, Bobbi Sloan, Sayre Van Young, Lisa Krieshok, and Todd Hensley; to Walter Filling for his expert calligraphy; to Nancy Smith for careful manuscript advice and discussions on folklorists; to Gloria Allen for a decorative arts question answered; to all those who shared their quilts; to Lee Porter for her generosity and open differing of opinion; to Sue Hannan and Jan Sheridan and their husbands for a helping hand; to Pamela Reising, Susan McKelvey, and the Lunch Bunch (Kathie, Lois, and Ellen) for encouragement; to the Schoolhouse Quilters who created Lafayette Elementary School's raffle quilt without me this year; to Mike Frye for patient computer aid; and to Marge Dowsett of Annapolis for the visit with her ancestral Album Quilt Blocks.

Thank you to my parents-in-law, Claudia and Alexei Sienkiewicz, for enabling me to travel to teach; to my children, Donald, Alex, and Katya, who helped more and for longer during this book; and to my husband, Stan, who supported me so well throughout.

*Dedicated to Mummy and Grandma, who taught me to sew; to my
West Virginia aunts, Atha, Orpha, and Gladys, and Cousin Wilma,
who gave me a love for quilts; to Aunt Betty who quilts along with me;
and to my husband and children who give me reasons to make quilts.*

Author's Preface

Thank you for joining me on our journey to Baltimore and beyond. The mid-nineteenth century in America was the heydey both of appliqué and of appliquéd Album Quilts. The Baltimore Album Quilts as a group are so striking, so recognizable, and so numerous that for me they serve as a classic standard, that is, a standard which serves as a model of design excellence. From these classic quilts[1] we can learn the techniques of a time and place where Appliqué was Queen.

Baltimore Beauties and Beyond, Studies in Classic Album Quilt Appliqué, is primarily a basic text on how to appliqué. Inevitably, it becomes a firsthand study of the Baltimore Album Quilts as well. The patterns herein are either faithfully reproduced from classic Baltimore Album Quilts or are "Beyond Baltimore" in space or time, but in keeping with Baltimore style. I have labeled each pattern presented as either "Baltimore" or "Beyond." Where I have modified a classic block, I've noted this, for it seems in all our interests to label "Baltimore" only those which are documented as classic Baltimore.

The techniques covered here are also both "Baltimore" and "Beyond." For while traditional cutwork appliqué[2] rekindled my passion for hand appliqué, once I had used such techniques as "freezer paper on top," I could never return completely to the nineteenth-century mode. Finding that every appliqué devotee is convinced that her way is best, I have included as many different appliqué techniques as I could work into *Baltimore Beauties'* twelve lessons. Within these pages can be found, I'm sure, your favorite appliqué method.

Baltimore Beauties and Beyond is the first of three how-to volumes based on these classic quilts. It is our "packed bag," containing all we need to set out on our journey to that Mecca of Classic Appliqué, mid-nineteenth-century Baltimore. Once there, we'll sew with our needlesisters of yore, the good "Ladies of Baltimore.[3]" Some of us will linger there, others will continue their journey beyond Baltimore.

In this first volume of *Baltimore Beauties*, the focus is on the block unit of the Baltimore Album Quilt: learning its design characteristics and how

to make it. The color plates exhibit the Lesson Blocks, plus exceptional antique and contemporary "Baltimore Beauties" which support the lessons. Other aspects of appliqué Album Quiltmaking, including more blocks, sets, borders, and quilting patterns for these classic quilts, are in *Baltimore Beauties, Volume II,* and *More Baltimore Beauties, Volume III.* I hope you will continue your journey in those volumes as well.

The richness of these Album Quilts is both visual and intellectual. We need to understand both aspects if we aspire to convey as much, as beautifully, as they did. Their meanings intrigue us as much as their beauty,[4] for it is in the nature of being a quiltmaker to be a folklorist as well. The folklorist preserves and passes on the material evidence of a culture and seeks to interpret it. So have quiltmakers ever done.

Like us, the makers of these classic quilts held hands with the past while pointing to the future. Steadfastly they incorporated older designs and techniques. Brilliantly they innovated in style and spoke through their quilts of specific lives and times.[5] Quiltmakers are both the "folk" and the folklorists. We make quilts and pass the culture on. While preserving our roots, we try to understand the meaning of what we do.

We cherish old patterns and old techniques, both for themselves and for what they tell us about our nation, our art, and ourselves. The tradition of our craft is passed on, but we change it with the flavor of our own lives. Some of us are consumed with the stuff of tradition. Others of us, a Nancy Crow or a Michael James, securely grounded in this rich heritage, take wing and break new frontiers. We recognize these traits in our sisters of bygone Baltimore as we do in each other today.

The decorative, realistic, Victorian design style in these classic Album Quilts was so distinctive that it broke new frontiers. It was a major factor in setting the Baltimore Album Quilts apart in a period profuse with appliqué Album Quilts. Today we call these quilts classic. I am convinced that the style of these classic quilts can be learned: both its design characteristics and the methods of its construction. Moreover, its rich Victorian modes of expression—pictures, words, and symbols—are knowable.

How lucky we are to be able to ply the needlepath, to some extent, of those who created these classic quilts. Use these lessons as a map. Guidebook in hand, you can visit bygone Baltimore. Some of you will find classic appliqué so congenial, so nourishing to your personal aesthetic, that you will inevitably travel far beyond Baltimore. And one or two among you may set a new classic standard, that of the Baltimore Album Quilt Revival of the late twentieth century.

However far your journey takes you, I hope *Baltimore Beauties* equips you well: first to follow skillfully, then perhaps to lead. Above all, enjoy yourself, be yourself, for thus are masterpiece quilts ever born.

NOTES

[1] I have chosen to call "classic" that period of quilts (about 1843-45 through 1852) included in the Baltimore Museum of Art's 1980-82 exhibition of Baltimore Album Quilts.

[2] Common usage of needlework terms is in a confusing state. The same name for a technique can mean different things to different people. "Cutwork," for example, is, by one definition, the embroidery method of buttonholing fabric, then cutting away the intervening cloth. Another usage, as Charlotte Patera uses it in *Cutwork Appliqué*, means cutting an appliqué a bit at a time, only as it is ready to be seamed under. For brevity, I am using "cutwork" in this latter usage. Charlotte herself has, more recently, in *Quilter's Newsletter Magazine*, #199, referred to this same method as "cut-away appliqué."

[3] In the impressively researched Baltimore Museum of Art catalog, *Baltimore Album Quilts*, Dena Katzenberg develops the theory that the style of a particular woman, Mary Evans, is distinctive in the Baltimore Album Quilts and attributes specific quilts to her. Referring to Mary Evans' quilting group, Katzenberg writes, "It is the author's further hypothesis that the wealthy Mrs. [Acsah Goodwin] Wilkins acted as patroness, supplying money or fine materials and the use of her home to the quilters. She is also convinced that Mary Evans may have been a protegé of the older woman, and that they were both members of a group who called themselves Ladies of Baltimore." She goes on to theorize that "a group of Methodist women worked together under the aegis of Acsah Wilkins, with the exceptional talents of a professional quilter, Mary Evans, to draw upon." She also connects Elizabeth W. Morrison with the group (p. 65).

Moreover, Katzenberg suggests, "Acsah Wilkins' influence on a number of Methodist women who were interested in quilting effected what was essentially a stylistic revolution.... Her example and precepts encouraged the development of a more refined and elegant style, identifiable by the use of a range of sophisticated imported materials, greater complexity of design, more proficient needlework, and multilayering or appliquéing of cloth for special effects" (p. 64).

[4] For a detailed discussion of meanings pictured, written, and symbolized in these quilts, see *Spoken Without a Word*.

[5] Religious sentiments, mainly Christian, thread through these quilts. Quilt #3 is a rare Jewish Bride's Quilt. Block C-4 shows a *chuppah* (wedding canopy) above a table bearing a *kiddush* cup and candles. Religion, politics, and the insignia of personal lives speak to us clearly throughout the Baltimore Album Quilts.

How to Use This Book

Use *Baltimore Beauties* as a workbook. Each lesson builds upon the previous lesson with increasingly complex skills presented. Begin with Lesson 1, then work your way through the twelve lessons in order.

"Part One: Getting Started" gives important information on design characteristics of the classic Baltimore Album Quilts, and covers fabric, tools, pattern transfer, and block preparation. Skim this material first, and refer back to it as needed for each lesson.

In "Part Two: The Lessons," each Lesson Block is described, and detailed sewing instructions are given. Patterns for each block are noted, and can be found by pattern number in "Part Four: The Patterns." For each Lesson Block you will need:

1. A 16" square of background fabric.

2. Cloth for the appliqués with thread to match. For Lessons 1 through 4, which have appliqués made from one single fabric, you will need one 16" square each of the appliqué fabric as well as of the background fabric.

A full-color close-up photo of each Lesson Block is shown in the Color Section to help you select your appliqué fabric.

The Gallery Quilts, also in the Color Section, exhibit eight quilts: four antique and four contemporary. Throughout this book, when a quilt is referred to by number (as quilt #4, or quilt #7), you will find it pictured in the Color Section. And, if you are wondering about the needleartists who worked on the contemporary quilts pictured, see "Part Three: The Quiltmakers."

When a specific block is referred to, for example, as "quilt #4, block E-2," the block can be located by its letter and number: the letters refer to the block position in the quilt, reading from left to right, and the numbers refer to position from top to bottom.

Part One: Getting Started

FABRIC

Block size and yardage requirements:
In the mid-nineteenth century, as now, many appliqué Album Quilts were not completely pre-planned. Thus, you can begin by making one block at a time. Give yourself the option to choose the finished size of the block and the quilt's set when you are further along.

The patterns in *Baltimore Beauties and Beyond* are all drafted for a 12 1/2" finished block size, but cut your background blocks 16" square to start. This allows room for correction should the appliqués become slightly misaligned on the block. Or, if you decide finally to set the blocks next to each other, this extra size allows more white space.

Two quilts, #6 and #7 in the color section, have 12 1/2" blocks set with sashings. This block size was taken from a classic 1847-50 Baltimore Album Quilt.[1] I chose this particular classic size because it allows you to add sashing and borders without the quilt getting too big. Since the typical Baltimore Album Quilt has five or more blocks across, block size is an important consideration.

Because *Baltimore Beauties and Beyond, Volume I*, concentrates on blocks alone, no specific yardages are given, beyond the simple advice to "buy plenty." Your quilt concept may change as you progress. Some blocks may be put aside for the next quilt, or new blocks may be needed to complete your design. Allow yourself enough background fabric for maneuvering. Ten yards of background fabric should be ample. In purchasing fabric, I estimate that the border's width is the same width as a block.

Background fabric:
In the classic Album Quilts, a high-quality off-white 100% cotton (not muslin) dominates. Because so many Album Quilts then, as now, were group projects, background fabric can differ within a given quilt. Even a tiny print background can be found among the otherwise solid neutral background fabrics in one square on an 1846-47 Baltimore Album Quilt.[2]

In quilt #7, I mixed off-white sheeting, both plain and tea-dyed, with flower-sprigged muslin. Background fabric now, as then, is thus clearly a matter of choice. Note here that an off-white background cloth highlights bright white appliqués in a way that a plain white background would not.

Appliqué fabrics:
The colors which dominate the antique Album Quilts are Turkey red and Victoria green on off-white. Look at these colors as well as the unique prints used in the antique Album Quilts, quilts #1 through #4 in the color section. Yellow seems to be the most common accent color. There is an impressive amount of pink in certain ornate Victorian Baltimore quilts as well, quilt #2 being one of them. This red/green color scheme allows a surprising variety in the total quilt look. Compare, for example, the brighter, clearer red/green look of quilt #6 with the more grayed decorator look of quilt #7.

Cotton prints dominate the appliqué fabric in these quilts. Many quilts are mainly calico. Quilts #3 and #4 are good classic examples. Certain sophisticated prints and print usage typify blocks/quilts that are connected in *Baltimore Album Quilts* to the Methodist quilters. Most recognizable are the "rainbow fabrics" which shade from light to dark in watercolor effect (Photo 1). Sometimes there is a floral motif or ripple print over the shaded background.

The typically clever use of prints includes a calico flower brightening a bird's eye, printed circles forming floral centers or the stylized stem indentation on fruit, printed flowers mixing with layered ones, and vases being framed by cutouts from anthemion prints. Small geometrics provided bricks for buildings or, on apple green, leaves and stems with ready-made turn lines. See

PHOTO 1. Block A-3 from the Metropolitan Museum of Art's Baltimore Album Quilt (shown in Photo 26). The squirrel is appliquéd from the same monochromatic floral-printed brown rainbow fabric as the center block's dove in Lee Porter's quilt #4. This particular fabric is used extensively in several classic Baltimore Album Quilts. (Photo: The Metropolitan Museum of Art: Sansbury Mills Fund. 1974.24)

quilts #1 through #4, then Albertine Veenstra's block (shown as enlarged detail of quilt #6), and Sylvia Pickell's ornate Victorian-style blocks (B-4, D-3, and D-4 in quilt #6) for comparably ingenious contemporary fabric use.

Some of the makers of the classic Baltimore Album Quilts were blissfully creative in choosing and embellishing fabric. Silk, silk velvet, wool embroidery, chintz, cotton prints of varying weights, ink, and even watercolors can be found in the classic quilts. Neither durability nor washability were foremost in their minds: they were creating art. Perhaps because these quilts were conceived and cherished as art, we are able still to enjoy them, almost a century and a half later.

The "Classic Look":

What characterizes the "Classic Look?" We need to answer this question if we are to go Beyond Baltimore, while keeping a recognizably Baltimore Album look. You may want a quilt in your favorite decorating colors. If so, ask yourself, "What, besides the actual colors (red/green/off-white, etc.) characterizes the 'Classic Look'?" Some or all of the following typify the Classic Look:

1. The Classic Look is well-defined: it has high-contrast colors on a pale solid field. Kate Fowle and I chose the fabric for quilt #8 to go with Mary Sue Hannan's dusty rose and blue color scheme. To keep the Classic Look, we picked the lightest of gray backgrounds, the darkest of blues, even touches of rose pushed to red, and the same bright splashes of yellow accent as are found in the quilt's red/green prototype (*New Discoveries in American Quilts*, p. 84). Compare the antique quilts (quilts #1 through #4 in the color pages) with the contemporary ones (quilts #5 through #8) to see how the classic style has been incorporated in those quilts that go "Beyond Baltimore."

2. There is an "airiness," a lot of background showing, throughout the classic appliqués. Their makers were not ladies afraid of stems and leaf-points, nor should anyone be. Quilts designed entirely or predominantly in the style linked in *Baltimore Album Quilts* to the Mary Evans/Acsah Wilkins/Lizzie Morrison group have a wonderfully spacious quality. To me, this is beautifully illustrated by quilt #1, although its Star Medallion center is unique.

PHOTO 2. Elegant block cut from one piece of fabric. These paper-doily-like blocks beautifully incorporate the German *scherenschnitte* design influence and the British Isles whole-cloth appliqué tradition into the classic Album Quilts. "From a circa 1852 Baltimore Album Quilt made for Miss Isabella Battee." (Photo: The Baltimore Museum of Art: Bequest of Queena and Belle Stewart, Buffalo Gap, South Dakota. BMA 1977.30)

PHOTO 3. Folded block design "from circa 1847-50 Baltimore Album Quilt made by Mrs. Mary Everist." This paper-cut design, possibly of oak leaves, is entirely buttonholed (except for the appliquéd center inscribed "Mary Physick") in light-colored sewing-weight thread. Both the quilt itself and this block reflect the passion for whole-cloth appliqué in Turkey red or green on white apparent in so many of the classic Album Quilts. (Photo: The Baltimore Museum of Art: Gift of Dr. William Rush Dunton, Jr., Baltimore. BMA 1946.159)

3. There are three types of block patterns in the classic Album Quilts; they appear both separately or combined:

   a. Two- to three-color patterns: These include both Victorian designs (sometimes asymmetrical) and patterns from an earlier time. Early border motifs such as dogtooth triangles, steps, scallops, peonies, swags ("hammocks") with bows/tassles/flowers, or fleurs-de-lis are common. Quilt #8 gives a grand display of several of these motifs in its borders. The 1852 prototype for this "Beyond Baltimore" quilt was passing on designs from at least as far back as 1790.[3]

   b. Folded paper-cut patterns: In these, the dominant color is cut all as one unit from a piece of cloth. These may show both British whole-cloth appliqué-style influences and German *scherenschnitte* ("paper-cuttings") influence.[4] See Photos 2 and 3 for examples.

   c. The more realistic Victorian patterns: These comprise the more elaborate layered blocks including the style in quilts attributed in *Baltimore Album Quilts* to Mary Evans, picture blocks (Photos 1, 4, 5, and 6), and Victorian versions of earlier blocks.[5] "Balanced a-symmetry" seems to have been sought after in much Victorian block design. Examples of it can be seen in blocks B-4, D-1, and D-4 of quilt #6.

These three pattern types vary, too, in the time it takes to make them. A simple cutwork block like "Double Hearts," Pattern #2, takes a single-minded needlewoman six to eight hours, while skilled professionals Sylvia Pickell, Donna Collins, and Cathy Berry report forty to sixty sewing hours on a "Mary Evans-style" block. This confirms my own experience with this book's cover blocks. As well as taking less time, the simpler blocks set the more complex ones off nicely. For examples of this effect, see quilts #2, #6, and #7.

Analysis of this mid-nineteenth-century "Classic Baltimore Album Quilt Look" enables us to develop a standard to aspire to, and by which other appliqué albums can be judged. This style can be studied, learned, and used as a wonderfully expressive design tool for our contemporary "Beyond Baltimore" Appliqué Album Quilts.

PHOTO 4.
"Basted quilt square of the City Springs" attributed by Arthur Evans Bramble to his great aunt, Mary Evans, as recorded by Dr. Dunton. Notice the illustrations (trees, railings, fence) drawn in the center of the block even before it has been sewn. (Photo: The Baltimore Museum of Art: William R. Dunton, Jr. Notebooks)

PHOTO 5.
Ornate Victorian Baltimore-style lyre wreath framing Baltimore's monument to George Washington. "From a circa 1852 Baltimore Album Quilt made for Miss Isabella Battee." This block is the prototype for our back cover block of the Statue of Liberty. (Photo: The Baltimore Museum of Art: Bequest of Queena and Belle Stewart, Buffalo Gap, South Dakota. BMA 1977.30)

PHOTO 6.
An ornate Victorian Baltimore-style broken wreath of layered flowers surrounds a steamship inscribed "Captain Russell." From an 1852 Baltimore Album Quilt, this block inspired the basic wreath pattern for our front cover block, Silhouette Wreath. (Photo: The Baltimore Museum of Art: The Hooper, Strauss, Pell and Kent Funds. BMA 1971.36.1)

I'm occasionally asked how quilts which incorporate different pattern types relate to those quilts composed entirely of ornate Victorian blocks. Is one type the true "Baltimore Album" style, and others not? No. They were all part of the appliqué Album Quilt boom of the mid-nineteenth century experienced in Baltimore and up and down the Eastern Seaboard. But in Baltimore there were identifiable differences. A phenomenal number of quilts from this period have the "look" of Baltimore and/or its name inscribed upon them.

The Baltimore Museum's Album Quilt Show catalog contains quilts from 1843-45 through 1852. I have chosen to label this rough time frame "the Classic Baltimore Album Quilt Period." Its quilts are the subject of our study of classic appliqué. Within these years we may see the emergence of a particularly skilled needlewoman, Mary Evans,[6] influencing Baltimore quilts. We see both the evolution of the ornate, more realistic Victorian style and its imitation. Certainly we see the contributions of other gifted needleartists as well in the quilts.

My personal belief is that Mary Evans, as we know her by a distinctive style only, may have been a designer and/or possibly a prototype seamstress for a designer. Time alone precludes her from being the primary needleartist designing and appliquéing the now dozen upon dozen quilts and blocks attributed, in the quiltmaking world, to her. The name "Mary Evans" has, by common usage among contemporary quiltmakers, come to stand for a *design style* which we can observe, even though the person and how many "Mary Evans' quilts" she is responsible for is clouded by time. She personalizes our link to these heirlooms of bygone Baltimore and invests us even more enthusiastically in trying to understand them.

One can't help but identify with the makers of the original Baltimore Album Quilts as one works through the lessons in this book. Lesson 12, "The 'Mary Evans' Challenge," shares some of my thoughts about who made these quilts, and I am anxious to hear your thoughts as well.

OTHER SUPPLIES AND EQUIPMENT

For pattern transfer:
You'll need a lightbox, dressmaker's carbon (also called "dressmaker's tracing paper"), tracing wheel, plastic-coated freezer paper, colored sewing thread, permanent pens (size .01 or .05),

mechanical pencil (size .05), stapler, staple remover, and "repositionable" tape (available at office supply stores).

Pins:
For cutwork, small straight pins which don't jab you as you hand sew are best. Sequin pins and pleater pins fill this job nicely. I have come to use the little 3/4" brass-plated safety-pins for virtually all my appliqué. Using them is quicker than basting and they stay put.

Scissors:
For appliqué and for paper-cutting, I prefer 5" tailor-point scissors. I find these strong enough for precision cutting of paper-foldings. Cutting to the point cleanly is very important for cutwork appliqué. The ideal situation is to have two pairs of 5" scissors and tag one "paper only."

Needles:
It is important to use Sharps, which are longer than the short Betweens beloved for quilting. The length of the Sharp needle makes it a critical tool for all needleturn appliqué. My favorite is Sharps #11. Beading needles and millinery needles are also excellent for appliqué. As with quilting needles, the size goes down as the number goes up. The double-ended needle-threader is fine enough to thread all these needles.

Thread:
It is the contemporary style for appliqué to be done in thread which matches the appliqué fabric in color. For purposes of hiding your stitches, if you can't get the exact match, choose a shade darker rather than lighter. Machine-weight thread is used. I particularly enjoy using three types of thread currently available: 100% cotton machine embroidery thread, 100% silk thread, and silk-covered cotton.

Permanent pens:
For adding signatures and embellishments, I have used the Pilot SC-UF™ Pen and the Pigma™ .01 and .05 in brown. Of course, always test the pen you use on your fabric first.

Light and magnification:
Good light and proper magnification are very important to appliqué. There are all sorts of wonderful devices available, from something as simple as the magnifying half-glasses sold at the drugstore (your optometrist can tell you the strength you

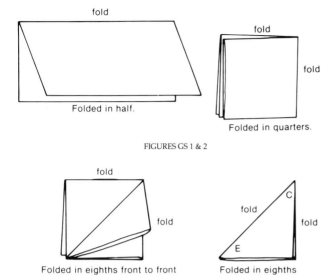

fold

Folded in half.

FIGURES GS 1 & 2

fold

fold

Folded in quarters.

fold

fold

Folded in eighths front to front
and back to back.

fold

fold

C

E

Folded in eighths
and marked.

FIGURES GS 3 & 4

need) to fluorescent-lit magnifying glasses which hang around your neck or clamp onto your table. If you are able to see clearly enough to thread your tiny needles, you are seeing well enough for heirloom appliqué.

PATTERN TRANSFER

There are two basic approaches to transfering the block pattern to your appliqué fabric and/or your background fabric: template methods and non-template methods. Both methods require that you first reproduce the block pattern from this book onto a 12 1/2" square of paper. "Part Four: The Patterns" is divided into patterns shown on one, two, or four pages. Transfering of these three pattern types is each based on a different variation of the following paper-folding method.

How to paper-fold in preparation for pattern transfer:

Use freezer paper for this. It is the right size, inexpensive, readily available, and thin enough both for folding and for tracing. Beyond this, its fine plastic coating adheres to fabric when ironed and can be peeled off when it's cooled off. Kate Fowle, of Washington, D.C., strongly recommends Reynolds™ brand freezer paper for use in appliqué.

Use a hot, dry iron (cotton to linen setting). Iron on a hard surface such as a breadboard or a fabric bolt cardboard core. Press firmly, and be careful

not to scorch. You can "heat baste" by pressing the iron's tip (only) down at desired intervals. Never spray starch your cloth first as the starch impairs adhesion.

If your freezer paper pattern lifts up, it can be ironed back down. Depending on the heat and pressure, a freezer paper template may be reusable. If you have any trouble removing the paper, plastic bag your project and put it in the freezer. The cold should contract the plastic coating of the freezer paper and make it "let go." Occasionally you may have to re-heat the paper with your iron, then scratch a last little bit off.

Fold a 12 1/2" square of freezer paper in the following manner. The flat, noncoated side should face out; the plastic coated side should face in.

1. Fold the square in half, folding top to bottom (Figure GS-1).

2. Fold the square into fourths, folding right to left (Figure GS-2).

3. Fold the square into eighths, folding the front to the front (Figure GS-3), and the back to the back (Figure GS-4).

4. Mark this eighth which faces you now. Mark "C" at the center where all the folds meet. Mark "E" in the lower left-hand corner for the "edges" (Figure GS-4 also).

How to take a pattern from this book:
There are three methods for taking patterns from this book, based on the number of pages that the pattern appears on in "Part Four: The Patterns."

FIRST METHOD: Patterns shown at one-quarter block on one page in "Part Four: The Patterns"

1. Fold and mark your pattern paper as in Steps 1 through 4, above. Now open up your folded square. Lay your "lettered" eighth over the pattern in the book, matching the "C" and "E" marks.

2. If your pattern is printed on a left-hand page, placement will look like Figure GS-5. If your pattern is on a right-hand page, placement will look like Figure GS-6.

3. For tracing, attach your folded paper to the pattern page with "repositionable" tape.

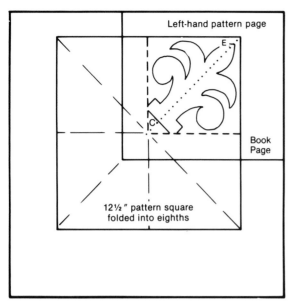

FIGURE GS-5

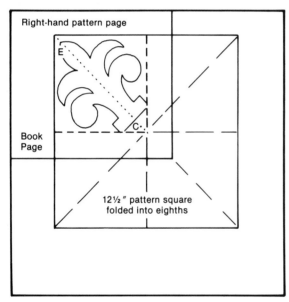

FIGURE GS-6

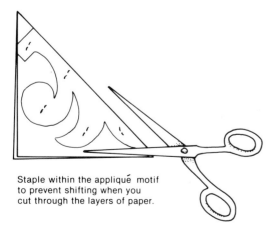

Staple within the appliqué motif
to prevent shifting when you
cut through the layers of paper.

FIGURE GS-7

4. Carefully trace one-eighth of the pattern. Hint: Although a quarter of the block is shown, you will get your most accurate pattern by tracing just an eighth of the block.

5. Refold your square into eighths. Staple in several places (within the drawn appliqué) to keep the layers from shifting while you cut (Figure GS-7). This helpful hint is from Jan Sheridan.

6. Cut out your folded and stapled appliqué pattern, remove the staples, and open up the template.

You can then transfer this freezer paper template by ironing it to the right side of your fabric and tracing around it. See Version I (drawing around freezer paper) below. Alternatively, you can work on a lightbox with the template placed under the appliqué fabric for tracing. Note: Patterns #4 and #11 are shown at one-quarter block but have special transfer instructions on their pattern pages.

SECOND METHOD: Patterns shown at one-half block on two pages in "Part Four: The Patterns"

1. Fold a 12 1/2" square of freezer paper into fourths. Mark "C" for the folded centers, "E" for the edges (Figure GS-8).

2. Using these fourths as guidelines, trace the pattern from the book's two pages onto the right-hand side of your freezer paper square (Figure GS-9).

3. To make a template, staple the right and left sides of the square together in several places, and cut the pattern out double (Figure GS-10).

If you want the whole pattern drawn out, rather than cut out, work on a lightbox. With the paper folded down the center, place the right-hand drawn side face down on the lightbox (Figure GS-11). Next trace that right half of the block pattern onto the left side of your square in a mirror image (Figure GS-12).

THIRD METHOD: Patterns shown as a whole block on four pages in "Part Four: The Patterns"

1. Fold a 12 1/2" square of freezer paper into fourths. Then number the fourths accord-

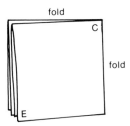

fold

fold

C

E

FIGURE GS-8

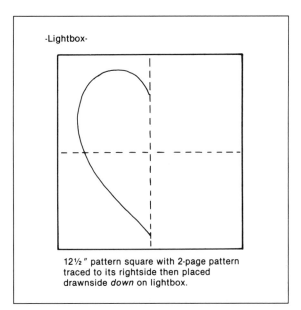

-Lightbox-

12½″ pattern square with 2-page pattern traced to its rightside then placed drawnside *down* on lightbox.

FIGURE GS-11

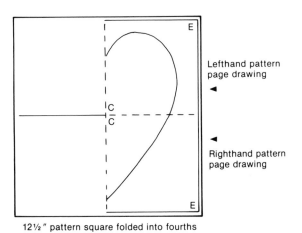

E

C
C

E

◄ Lefthand pattern page drawing

◄ Righthand pattern page drawing

12½″ pattern square folded into fourths

FIGURE GS-9

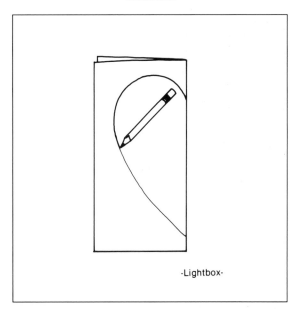

-Lightbox-

FIGURE GS-12

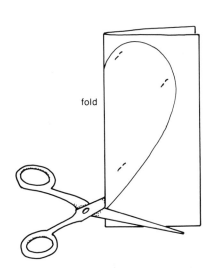

fold

FIGURE GS-10

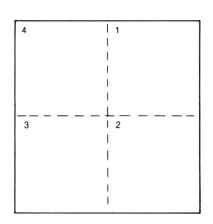

4	1
3	2

FIGURE GS-13

ing to the placement diagram at the top of the pattern pages (Figure GS-13).

2. Trace all four pages of the pattern from the book onto the freezer paper by quadrants.

How to transfer your pattern to fabric using a freezer paper template:

VERSION I (drawing around freezer paper):
The "Fleur-de-Lis" pattern from Lesson 1 is used as an example.

1. Iron the diagonals into your [red] appliqué fabric square as placement lines.

2. Using these lines as guides, center your freezer paper pattern ("Fleur-de-Lis") on the right side of your appliqué fabric with the flat-finished side of the paper facing you (Figure GS-14).

3. Heat baste your pattern in place. After ironing the paper cut-out down once lightly, flip the fabric over. Iron firmly from the wrong side. This way the paper pattern is underneath and won't get hooked by the iron.

4. With a fabric marker of your choice, trace around the freezer paper template (Figure GS-15). I like using a very fine permanent Pigma™ .01 pen in brown or black for this marking. It is clear and readable, but the marked fabric must be turned under completely when you appliqué.

5. When the appliqué fabric is completely marked, remove the freezer paper template.

VERSION II (freezer paper on top):
This method leaves the freezer paper template right on the top of the fabric. Rather than a drawn line, the paper's edge itself becomes the guideline for your appliqué turn line (Figure GS-16).

1. Iron the pattern very tightly to the right side of the appliqué fabric. Pay particular attention to points.

2. If the template is not tightly bonded, it will lift up as you appliqué, be a hindrance, and frustrate you unmercifully. A temporary pin-baste behind a point helps while you are sewing. Re-iron any loose areas when you get the chance.

16" square red fabric with diagonals ironed in for placement. Freezer paper template is heat-basted in place.

FIGURE GS-14

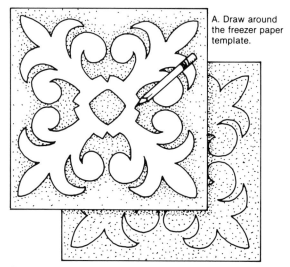

A. Draw around the freezer paper template.

B. After drawing, remove the freezer paper template. VERSION I —Drawing Around Freezer Paper.

FIGURE GS-15

Note for both versions: If your pattern is of separate units, not all one piece, simply cut them apart before ironing them down to the appropriate appliqué fabric. You will add your seam allowance to these patterns by eye as you cut out the shapes.

Other pattern transfer methods:
Tracing a pattern on a lightbox works well for appliqué fabric. Pin the pattern to the fabric first so that it doesn't shift, and use a clear, fine-line marker. Dressmaker's carbon paper also works well. It is specially formulated to wash out and comes in a variety of colors.

When you mark background fabric to assist in properly aligning the appliqués, use a lightbox with the pattern pinned underneath the background block. I make tiny dots with a Pigma™ .01 pen in brown. These rust-colored markings are so small they could be the flecks in muslin. Making as few dots as possible, I mark leaf points, corners, and outer wreath edges. Put such dots just inside the drawn turn line. This compensates for the shapes "shrinking" a bit as they are appliquéd down. More often, I do not mark at all, but pin my appliqués in place right on the lightbox where I can see their positions clearly.

Albertine Veenstra of Acton, Massachusetts, was taught never to make a mark on the background fabric. Instead, working on the lightbox, she baste-marks the background in the color thread of the appliqué to be placed there. Thus a stem would be marked in green running stitches, berry centers in red thread, etc.

BLOCK PREPARATION AND COMPLETION

Materials:
For each block, you need a 16" square of background fabric. For Lessons 1 through 3 you need a 16" square of the colored appliqué fabric for each block as well. Use a #11 Sharp needle with an 18" knotted thread in the color of your appliqué fabric.

Pin-basting:
Appliqués should always be securely pinned or basted to the background fabric. For cutwork appliqué you can quickly pin-baste:

1. Lay your pattern-marked appliqué fabric right side down on a table.

2. Center the background fabric on top of it. Safety pin-baste with just five pins: one in each corner and one in the center (Figure GS-17).

You will use two to three more pins, small straight pins preferably, in the immediate area where you are appliquéing. Move them as your work progresses. Always pin-baste from the back so that you don't catch your thread on the pins as you sew. This hint is from Charlotte Patera.

Pressing:
When the time comes to press your finished blocks, be sure to iron them from the wrong side. Place the block right side down on a fluffy terry towel so that the background cloth gets pressed,

VERSION II—Freezer Paper on Top

FIGURE GS-16

16" square red fabric, pattern-marked side face down on table. Background fabric is laid over it. Pin-baste in 5 places.

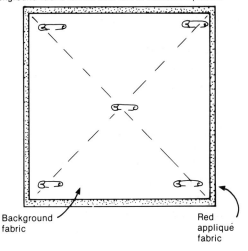

Background fabric   Red appliqué fabric

FIGURE GS-17

but the appliqués are not flattened, causing their seams to show through. Lay a white handkerchief over the back of the appliqué so that your iron does not catch on threads.

If you need to handwash a completed appliqué, or if you decide to tea-dye it, ironing it dry with paper towels on top may be a good idea. Some types of contemporary threads bleed and the paper towels seem to catch the color so that it does not stain the background fabric.

Cutting the block to size:
After pressing the completed appliqué, cut your block to size. If you choose to set the squares with sashing strips, you can cut them down to the 12 1/2" pattern size as follows:

1. Place the block wrong side up on a table or other workspace.

2. Position a transparent 12 1/2" plastic template, centered, over the appliqués so that their stitched outlines show. Secure the template with masking tape.

3. Trace the sewing line around the template's edge.

4. Cut 1/4" beyond this line to leave the block's seam allowance (Figure GS-18).

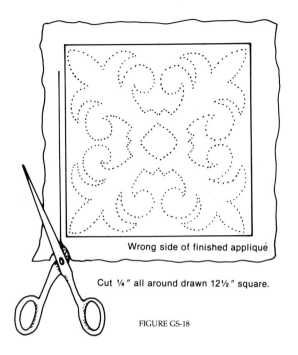

Wrong side of finished appliqué

Cut ¼" all around drawn 12½" square.

FIGURE GS-18

NOTES

[1] *Baltimore Album Quilts*, catalog #14 , p. 99.

[2] *Baltimore Album Quilts*, catalog #10 , p. 89, block G-5.

[3] English antecedents for these classic borders are illustrated in Averil Colby's *Patchwork*. On page 91 is an appliquéd marriage coverlet (circa 1790) with the "Fleur-de-Lis and Hammock" repeated in quilt #8. Colby notes (p. 75) that the double (four loop) bow border in this same coverlet is a pattern "used by Chippendale for ormulu [sic] mounts."

Multipart bows are used, seemingly with symbolic intent. The center medallion on Captain Russell's Presentation Quilt is single bow tied. The medallion on Elizabeth Sliver's Bride's Quilt is triple bow tied ("the lovers' knot"). The bow on a herald angel block dedicated to Reverend Robert Lipscomb has four tie ends, as though to form a Christian cross. (This block, B-2, is reproduced in quilt #6.)

[4] Cutting folded fabric freehand, without a template, was an earlier technique in both England and America. On the whole it created a "cookie-cutter look." Averil Colby notes that the finest English examples disappear after 1840.

There may be a bit of folded fabric cut appliqué in the classic Album Quilts, but the precision of the finest one-, two-, and thre-color blocks bespeak paper-cut patterns. Faithfully reproduced blocks in quilt #6 (blocks A-1, A-3, and A-5; B-3 (border); B-5; C-1 and C-5; D-5; and E-1, E-3, E-4, and E-5) seem clearly to me to have been paper template-cut.

[5] To illustrate, see the very symmetrical block E-2 in quilt #6. Compare this to the more fluid, asymmetrical Victorian-style grape vine wreath, block C-1 in quilt #7.

[6] Mary Evans (married name, Ford) is referred to in the Orlofsky's *Quilts in America* (1974) on page 239: "...enterprising seamstresses may have supplied quilt block patterns much as needlepoint experts today. It is also believed that a professional needlewoman living in Baltimore, Mary Evans Ford, may have produced a number of these beautiful Baltimore Album Quilts, possibly as bridal trousseau quilts, and as many as twenty-six."

Subsequent extensive research was published in *Baltimore Album Quilts* by Dena Katzenberg (Baltimore Museum of Art, Baltimore, 1981):

"An unfinished quilt block, one of a set of seven with pencil lines, and basted appliqués, was brought to the attention of the quilt expert, Dr. William Dunton by Arthur Evans Bramble. Bramble informed Dr. Dunton that the blocks were the work of his great aunt, Mary Evans.

"This piece established some of the hallmarks of Mary Evan's works: triple bowknots, prominent white roses, figures with inked features, the use of rainbow fabrics to indicate contour, a sure sense of formal design, and compositional skill. Such careful elegant work on so many quilts leads to the conclusion that a professional quiltmaker was at work. The author has identified over a dozen quilts which she considers to be the sole work of Mary Evans, and numerous individual blocks on other quilts." (*Baltimore Album Quilts*, pp. 61-62.) See Photo 4.

Mary Evans lived from 1829 to 1916 (*Ibid.*, p. 61). Her bricklayer father, Daniel Evans, died when she was 17. That year, 1846, is when quilts attributed to her in *Baltimore Album Quilts* began to appear (1846-52). It seems to me she would be a bit young for such far-reaching influence on her own. It is also not clear to me from published evidence alone that Mary Evans was necessarily more (a designer or influential organizer) than the person who was to stitch the blocks attributed to her by her nephew.

My sense is that the volume of contemporary popular attribution to Mary Evans distorts a bit the careful presentation of evidence in *Baltimore Album Quilts*. Dena Katzenberg's researches point to many influences including a Methodist church sewing circle. At this distance, the interaction of needleartists within the church and the group itself seem to me almost inseparable from any one particular talent.

In time, we may be able to trace, by evolving style if not by name, a handful of individual needleartists in the Methodists' Baltimore Album Quilts. Ms. Katzenberg is measured and concrete in linking the additional names Acsah Wilkins and Lizzie Morrison to the 1846-52 period in which she brackets the beginning and end of these classic quilts (*Baltimore Album Quilts*, p. 14). She gives the date 1853 when Lizzie Morrison's name is removed from the church rolls, and 1854 when Acsah Wilkins dies (*Ibid.*, p. 65). These dates are tantalizingly close to Katzenberg's end date for "the highly refined style" of the Baltimore Album Quilts. She seems, in fact, to be on the brink of finding out so much about who, why, and when. I hope that she--and you--will continue this unearthing of evidence and will share the evolving hypotheses with us all.

Part Two: The Lessons

Dot Reise, Severna Park, Md. March 1988

LESSON 1:

Cutwork Appliqué and the Tack Stitch (Both Visible and Hidden), 3/16" Seams, the Terms "In-laid" and "Onlaid" Appliqué, Mending Appliqué, and Troubleshooting Points and Corners

PATTERN:
"Fleur-de-Lis I," Pattern #1 (Photo 7)

Several years ago Charlotte Patera, author of the now out-of-print book *Cutwork Appliqué,* sent me a kind note saying that the Baltimore Album Quilt pattern, "Vine-Wreathed Heart," from my book *Spoken Without a Word,* was a perfect design for doing in cutwork appliqué. (See quilt #6, block C-1, and quilt #7, block D-2.)

Thank you, Charlotte. I took your advice, learned cutwork, fell in love with its speed of preparation and ease of execution, and then never stopped. I've applied cutwork appliqué to the simplest Album Quilt blocks and to complex Victorian-style blocks such as those on the covers of this book.

Cutwork is not the answer to every appliqué task, but it is a wonderful place to start. Like all appliqué, it improves with practice. As you work through the lessons, keep an open mind and see how different challenges call for different appliqué methods.

BLOCK PREPARATION/ PATTERN TRANSFER

Review "Part One: Getting Started," especially the sections on freezer paper transfer (Version I) and block preparation (for materials and pin-basting techniques).

CUTWORK APPLIQUÉ

The principles of cutwork are simple:

1. Make no cuts until you are ready to sew in a specific area. Then cut just up to 2" at a time. The crux of the method is to cut a little, sew a little. Repeat this until the block is finished.

2. Do not change the direction of your cut until you have completed all the sewing in one direction. This means you sew all the way up to an outward or inward point

PHOTO 7. "Fleur-de-Lis I," Pattern #1. Appliqué, pattern drafting, and fabric selection by Elly Sienkiewicz, 1988. (Photo: S. Risedorph)

before you change directions and tackle the other side.

This "one side at a time approach" takes the worry out of cutwork. Inward points become a matter of one straight line finished with a tight anchoring tack stitch, then you change directions and tackle another straight line. Outward points are also just one line at a time, as we shall see.

Cutwork is a homey lesson in postponed anxiety: Don't worry today about things you can't do anything about until tomorrow. Cutwork's comforting message is that the worry about all those points and hard places is most often worse than the task itself.

3. The uncut fabric helps you by holding the appliqué in place. It eliminates the need for extensive basting. As soon as it is hindering you, it is time to cut some more. Basting pins are there to help you. When they are hindering you, or are no longer holding the area where you are sewing, move them.

And what are the advantages of cutwork?

1. Speed of preparation means you simply trace your design, pin-baste, and you're ready to appliqué.

2. There's perfect alignment of all parts of the pattern, since no elements of the design are able to shift out of place.

3. The ease of appliqué means, because the whole process works to help you like a "third hand," you're able to concentrate on perfecting curves, points, and stitches.

APPLIQUÉ METHOD—ONE-COLOR CUTWORK APPLIQUÉ

To begin, determine where you will begin cutting into the appliqué fabric.

1. Always start at an outward (not an inward) point. If you are right-handed, you will begin to the left of the point. If you are left-handed, begin to the right of the point. With apologies to left-handers, convention is followed here and all further directions/diagrams are given for right-handers.

2. To do fine appliqué, you need to admit that you're a giant for this sort of thing and give yourself plenty of room. Make a nice long "handle" by which to turn any point under: Cut through the top (red) fabric only. Make a cut 3/16" parallel to the turn line as shown in Figure 1-1.

    Stop your cut 3/16" from the opposite edge's turn line. This 3/16" is a generous seam allowance, but not too bulky. You will get fine curves with it, and sharp concave corners. You will appreciate its real genius when it comes to flipping under your perfect points.

    Learning appliqué with tiny seams, and trying to turn both sides of tiny points under at once, is a recipe for frustration. If you've ever had a moment of appliqué discouragement, keep an open mind and follow these directions exactly. This method is a bit different, but it works phenomenally well. Later lessons will make modifications for even finer appliqué.

3. Add three more pins (behind the background fabric) to baste the immediate area where your appliqué begins (Figure 1-2).

Starting to sew:

4. Hold your fabric so that the seam is away from you (Figure 1-3). This allows your left thumb to help actively in smoothing the seam ahead of your needle. Pulling points under toward you is also much, much

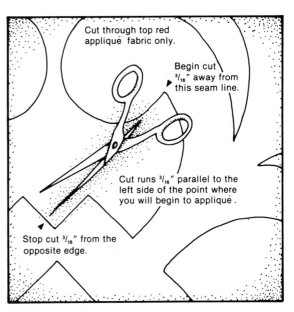

FIGURE 1-1

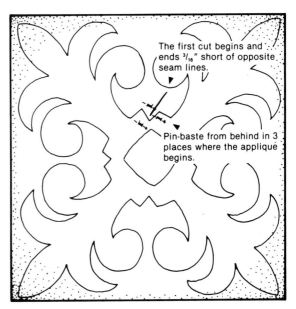

FIGURE 1-2

easier than pushing them under away from you.

Using your needle in your right hand, turn your seam allowance under in a nice straight line passing beyond the point (Figure 1-3, also). With your left thumb, press hard so that the turn line holds.

Securing the point:

5. Your needle enters the block from the back of the background fabric (the knot remains there). Push your needle up from the back of the background fabric and out through the appliqué's fold line right at the point

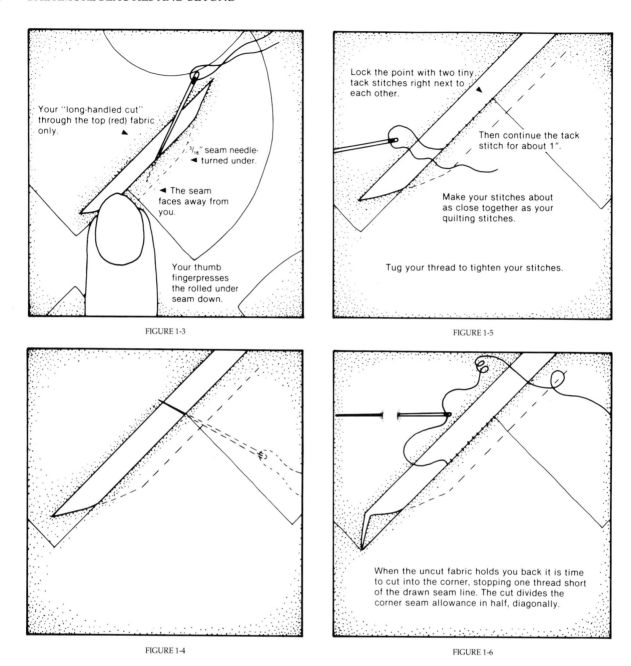

FIGURE 1-3

FIGURE 1-5

FIGURE 1-4

FIGURE 1-6

(where the two lines of the corner touch). See Figure 1-4.

Pull your thread tight. Take another tiny tight stitch right next to the first one, on its left. These two tiny tack stitches lock the point (Figure 1-5). (See the section on the tack stitch at lesson's end.) Always lock your points. This gives a nice tight seam against which to shove the right-hand seam allowance when, after sewing completely around the fleur-de-lis, you come back to finish this point (Figure 1-6). Continue sewing right to left for about half an inch with the tack stitch.

The concave or inward point:

6. When the uncut fabric is holding you back, it is time to cut into the concave corner. Your cut will bisect the corner exactly (giving equal seam allowance to both sides) and stop one thread short of the turn line (Figure 1-6).

    This cut looks at you with pristine, crisp edges. It isn't frayed. Tell yourself, "I have one or two chances to slide my seam allowances under smoothly. Only my fussing at that corner repeatedly is going to make it fray."

7. Don't use the fray-causing point, but rather the side of your needle to turn the corner under. Slip your needle about 1/3" under the appliqué. The needle's point and one-third of its length is between the background fabric and the appliqué; the rest of it is to the right above the appliqué with its side resting on the cut edge right at the corner (Figure 1-7).

8. Place your left thumb over the appliqué's corner and push down, sandwiching the seam between your thumb and your forefinger (which is behind the background fabric). Simultaneously pull the seam allowance under and towards you with the side of the needle. Fingerpress to crease in this folded-under corner seam.

   Withdraw the needle after turning the corner under. Don't lift up your thumb and look. Chances are 99% that you have turned a perfect corner, but if you haven't, there's no sense worrying about it until you sew up closer to the corner and can try again. Your conviction (and the pressure of your thumb) will help turn a perfect corner.

9. When you've tack-stitched up to your thumb, lift up your thumb to see the corner. If there is fray, see the section on "Troubleshooting" at the end of these instructions. Otherwise, tack-stitch right up to the corner. The last stitch in the corner you take twice, one stitch on top of the other (Figure 1-8).

   Let's walk through this corner stitch together. First, take a deeper bite out of the fabric, two to three threads deep because all you have is a raw edge. Then, take the stitch once. Next, reenter the background where you have just now entered it, and take the stitch again, as in Figure 1-8.

   Because the last stitches before a corner have little or no seam allowance, you don't want to pull your needle up perpendicularly towards your face on the exit from the fabric. This pulls the fragile edge up. Rather, encourage the rolling under process by exiting and reentering the fabric almost horizontally. Diane Elliott of Canada describes the process: "When you pull your needle out of the fabric, aim it directly across the room. When you reenter the fabric to complete the stitch, aim the needle directly towards your stomach. This rolls the seam under nicely."

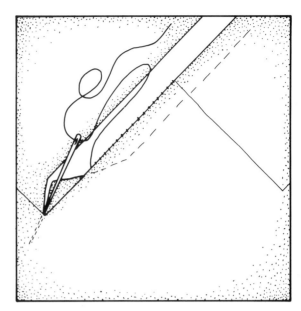

FIGURE 1-7

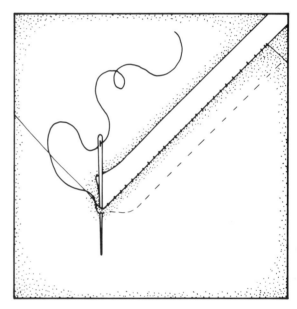

FIGURE 1-8

Cutting in the opposite direction—the left-hand side of the corner:

10. Cut 3/16" parallel to the turn line and out 1" beyond the next point in a straight line (Figure 1-9). This creates your "handle" for turning under the seams of the inward and outward points easily.

11. Needleturn under the left seam allowance on this inward corner. I find it always helps to start the turning under about an inch above where my stitches will begin. Anchor the appliqué at this point with your thumb. Just below it, use the side of the

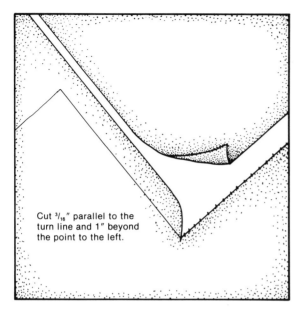

Cut ³/₁₆″ parallel to the turn line and 1″ beyond the point to the left.

FIGURE 1-9

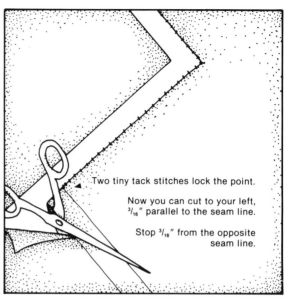

Two tiny tack stitches lock the point.

Now you can cut to your left, ³/₁₆″ parallel to the seam line.

Stop ³/₁₆″ from the opposite seam line.

FIGURE 1-11

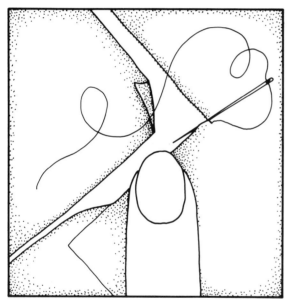

FIGURE 1-10

needle to catch the seam, tuck it under, and pull towards yourself with a sliding motion, turning under the seam allowance to the corner. Fingerpress tightly. Tack-stitch down the left side of the corner (Figure 1-10).

12. Sew up to the outward point. The last 1/3" before a point should be good tight close stitches. This prevents bulge when you tuck under the other side of the point. Take the last two stitches at the point right next

to each other. Pull these tight to "lock" the point.

Changing direction of the cut—flipping under the point:

13. Only after you've completed and locked the right side of the point do you cut in the opposite direction, down the left side of the point. Stop 3/16" from the opposite edge (Figure 1-11).

14. Cutwork points are done a special way which is almost failproof: Hook your needle's point into the appliqué and its seam allowance (Figure 1-12). The full 3/16" seam allowance makes grabbing these two layers easy.

    Push down (to keep your needle "loaded" with seam allowance), against, but not through, the background fabric and towards you. Swing the needle around until it is stopped by the right-hand seam which you've just sewn (Figure 1-13).

15. Voila! A perfect point. The seam allowance is lying flatly folded, smoothed clear across underneath the appliqué's point. Now quickly lock that point with one tight tack stitch (Figure 1-14).

Your goal was just to turn the point itself, and you did it perfectly. Now you can needleturn

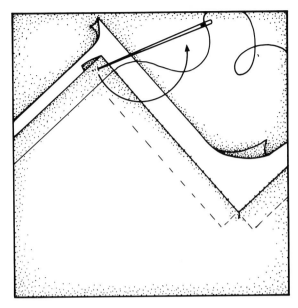

FIGURE 1-12

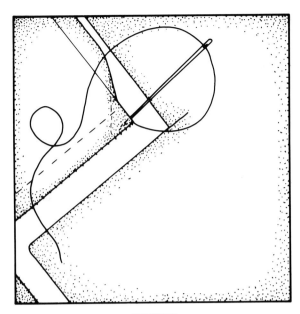

FIGURE 1-13

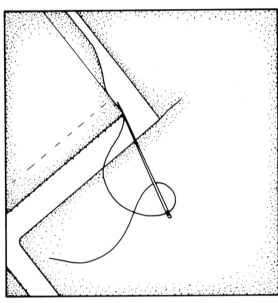

FIGURE 1-14

under the seam allowance for the straight seam ahead. There was no point in worrying how that seam would look when you weren't yet in a position to sew it, but now you are. Needleturn under the seam allowance and continue appliquéing.

If on this, your first try, you had some trouble on your perfect point, see the section on "Troubleshooting" toward the end of this lesson.

All the points on this pattern are done in the same way. All convex corners are done as in Steps 8 through 12. When you come to the inward points between the lily's petals, you have a more acute angle and thus less seam allowance (Figure 1-15). Simply split the difference between the right and left side when you cut. The worst that can happen is that you will take a bit more seam allowance than the pattern gives. Just do it with nice smooth lines and a "good eye." If appliqué looks right, it is right.

Figure 1-15 also shows where to clip on an inward curve. Clip only as needed (to two to four threads short of the turn line) to ease the curve. Too much or too deep clipping weakens the seam.

In cutwork appliqué there is no clipping on outward curves. The seam allowance is spread out smoothly underneath with a fanning motion by the needle.

For an appealing curve, always smooth and fingerpress about an inch ahead of where you are ready to sew. Anchor this prepared area with your left thumb. The secret to avoiding "peaks" in your beautiful curve? Never sew right up to your thumb. Always leave a bit (about 1/4") of the

prepared curve unsewn while you smooth out the next inch of curve. With this bit of advice, you now have the tools to complete everything except the center on your fleur-de-lis block. Enjoy!

THE CENTER OF THE FLEUR-DE-LIS— INLAID APPLIQUÉ

According to Averil Colby, "inlay" is the nineteenth-century term for what today we call "reverse appliqué." Inlaid appliqué turns in to reveal a bottom fabric; onlaid appliqué puts the appliquéd fabric on top. We have just been doing onlaid cutwork appliqué. These terms are so clear and descriptive that I will use them from this point on.

There is a slight tendency in cutwork appliqué to push the appliqué inward so that it "puffs" a bit. It works fine in onlaid appliqué, but not as well in inlaid appliqué where some distortion may occur. For success, baste around the block's center, 1/4" inside the turn line (Figure 1-16). Then go ahead and trim to the 3/16" seam allowance all around.

If you have time to complete this center in one sitting, begin with a diagonal corner cut. Otherwise, begin in the middle of one side so as not to leave a cut to the turn line raw and vulnerable to fray. Now, needleturn under the seam and appliqué this inlaid center just as you have been doing your onlaid appliqué on the rest of the block.

TROUBLESHOOTING

Convex corners:
If there's a bit of fray, make a judgment about whether you should, with the side of your needle, tuck it underneath the right seam allowance where you're sewing. Alternatively, you can sometimes sew right up to one last recalcitrant thread and then include it in "tomorrow's problems" when you change directions at the corner, tucking it under the next, left-hand, seam.

I've been asked if one can snip off one bit of fray. No. Use your thumb to stabilize the appliqué. Then use the back of your needle, use the point of your scissors, use a wooden toothpick, but get that thread bent under with as little consternation to the corner as possible.

Mending appliqué:
If a bit of fray emerges later, or if you see a bit of pucker, you can go back and mend your appliqué. Start the additional stitches a bit to the right of the problem area and finish a bit to its left. If the problem is a peak or a pucker, smooth it out by fanning the needle under the seam allowance. Sometimes fingerpressing this rearranged seam, even without stitches, restores a smooth curve.

It may help to lay your work on the table so that you have full use of both hands to cure a problem. Many people appliqué better with their hands resting on something anyway. I sew on a 10"-high picnic/sewing hamper so that the work

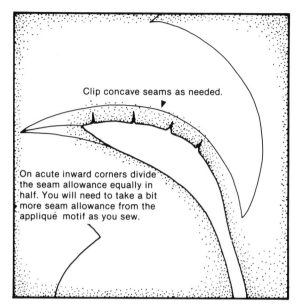

Clip concave seams as needed.

On acute inward corners divide the seam allowance equally in half. You will need to take a bit more seam allowance from the appliqué motif as you sew.

FIGURE 1-15

FIGURE 1-16

is raised to me, rather than my bending over to it, which strains my back and neck.

Points:
If by accident you cut too close to the point and don't have that nice, easy-to-flip-under 3/16" seam allowance, try this method. First, hold the appliqué between your left thumb and forefinger. Press the seam allowance down and away with your thumb. Don't use a needle, but instead try something less fraying such as embroidery scissor points or a round wooden toothpick to shove that

seam allowance under tightly between your thumb and forefinger. Hold it tight like that while you say a few magic words over it (fingerpress), then lock it in place with a tack stitch or two.

Points in general are vulnerable in appliqué. When a smaller seam allowance is used, it is wise to reinforce the points (from the back of the block) by taking several stitches on top of each other behind the points. (This hint is from Albertine Veenstra who repairs antique quilts and notes that points are about the most frequently damaged areas.)

THE TACK STITCH

This is a strong and versatile stitch, one frequently used in the classic Baltimore Album Quilts (and mid-late nineteenth-century appliqué in general). While we'll go on to learn other stitches, you could happily stop with this one.

In the nineteenth century, the tack stitch was commonly done in white or a neutral color thread. It was often quite visible, as though it were the style to show these tiny, staple-like stitches strung out in neat rhythmic strokes at the appliqué's edge (Figure 1-17). Some of the classic Baltimore Album Quilt blocks are done with a more hidden tack stitch, and that is the one we'll strive for.

The tack stitch is basically a staple. It comes from the back up through the folded-under seam allowance and out through the top fabric. To best hide it, we want the stitch very short and straight. Thus, when your needle comes out through the top fabric, swing it away from your body and exit out the fold rather than taking a longer, more visible "bite" out of the appliqué (Figure 1-18).

To reenter the background fabric, put your needle back into the hole your thread just came out of. I find it easiest to do this by slipping my needle point under the folded edge to reenter the background fabric just behind the exit stitch (Figure 1-19). You complete this stitch in the same motion that begins the next stitch: swing the point away from you and back out the appliqué's fold.

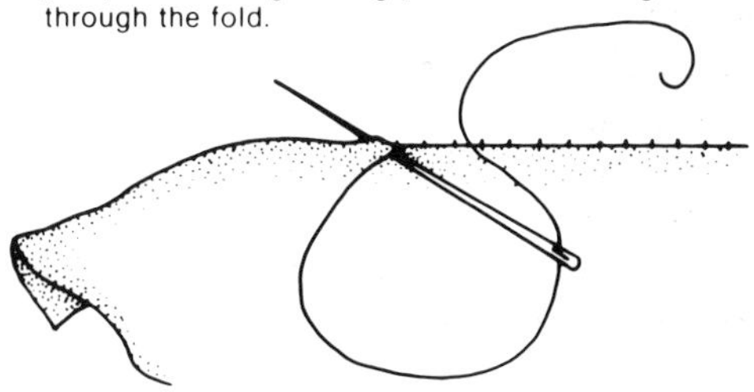

The stitch you've just made is really just a tiny loop from the edge of the fold back into the hole you came out of. All forward progress is made underneath the block.

Your tack stitch should be virtually invisible. It doesn't show atop the appliqué because it comes out the fold, and it doesn't show on the background fabric because it enters this cloth hidden

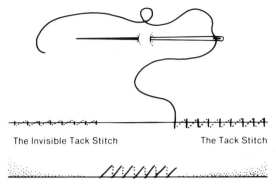

The Invisible Tack Stitch   The Tack Stitch

The Visible Tack Stitch
Nineteenth-century
Style

FIGURE 1-17

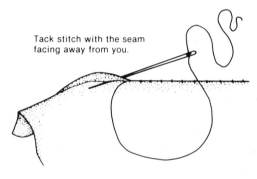

Tack stitch with the seam
facing away from you.

FIGURE 1-18

Put your needle in just behind the stitch you've just pulled through. Bring your needle out right through the fold.

FIGURE 1-19

underneath your appliqué. But the question remains, how close together should the stitches be? One class participant gave this good general answer—"as close as your quilting stitches. This allows for personality differences."

In actual fact, you have to take close stitches at the tips of points so that they don't bulge or fray. When you are needleturning under the seam as in cutwork, you have to take stitches close together on tight curves.

On long curves or straight lines you can allow more space between stitches and go faster. Your judgment for this comes with practice. No one will know how practical you've been unless the quilt remains unfinished and the appliqué's back can be seen. (First aid for exhausted appliqué artists is listed in Appendix I, under "Commissioned Quilting and Binding.")

How many stitches:
Beautiful appliqué is done at seven to ten tack stitches per inch, counting just those showing on top. Extremely fine appliqué runs seventeen to twenty stitches per inch. The strength of your appliqué is affected by both the closeness of the stitch and the width of the seam allowance. Tiny seam allowances need closer stitches; wider ones allow less close stitches. Since we're starting with a generous 3/16" seam, our stitches can run to the "beautiful" (seven to ten per inch) and our concentration should be more on making them hidden than on making them excruciatingly close together.

More about hiding stitches:
Using the same thread color as the appliqué fabric makes hiding the stitches easier. Fine thread (silk or 100% cotton machine appliqué thread) as well as tightly pulled thread helps hide your stitches.

Ending your thread in appliqué:
There are several methods for ending your thread in appliqué: several stitches sewn on top of each other inside the back edge of an appliqué, or a loop knot or two over a seam's stitch on the back of the quilt, or a tight back-stitch with the knotted thread end hidden inside a seam. Starting knots can be similarly hidden inside a seam. (Rather than worry overmuch about this, I prefer to look forward to a finished quilt where one's knots are inevitably hidden forever.)

The tack stitch can be done with the seam you are sewing facing you or the seam facing away from you. On this cutwork block, the appliqué should be facing toward you and the seam facing away. This arrangement has the advantage that points are easy to turn, and the surmountable disadvantage for us of having to work a bit harder to hide our stitches. We'll return to this discussion of the two directions of appliqué in Lesson 3.

Another pattern to make using onlaid cutwork: "Double Hearts," Pattern #2. This project is classic, quick, and easy enough for a beginner.

LESSON 2:

Onlaid Cutwork Appliqué with Freezer Paper on Top, Plus Pattern Bridges and the Blind Stitch (Alias the Invisible Appliqué Stitch, the Ladder Stitch, the Pumpkin Stitch, the Jack-o'-Lantern Stitch, the Slip Stitch, the Speed Stitch, and the Hem Stitch)

PATTERN:
"Wreath of Strawberry Leaves," Pattern #22 (Photo 8)

In the Victorian's "language of the flowers," strawberry leaves meant completion or perfection.[1] This makes them wonderfully appropriate for our second cutwork lesson, for this pattern poses an inward or an outward point every inch or so. And as the road to perfection is paved with practice, you'll get plenty of it on this charming wreath. Upon completion, you will surely have attained perfection.

We're now adding a nontraditional element to the cutwork method covered in detail in Lesson 1. There we traced around our freezer paper template to mark the appliqué turn line, then removed the paper. This time we are going to leave the freezer paper on, using the cut edge of the design to mark the seam edge. Though perhaps a bit awkward at first, the "freezer paper on top" method has such advantages that it is well worth pushing yourself to learn this technique.

First, what are the advantages? With the "freezer paper on top" method, pattern transfer time is cut (you need only the time to smooth the pattern on with an iron). Second, the appliqué is kept smooth and flat by the paper, and a highly visible, stiff, sharp edge is presented to needleturn your seam allowance under against. Third, the freezer paper acts as a "third hand" holding the appliqué edge down flat as you tuck the seam back underneath it.

You can hold fabric/freezer paper rolled up in your hand just as you would if the paper were not there. You will be sewing just beyond (about 1/32") the freezer paper's edge, so that you can see what you're doing. The only frustration is that the freezer paper can lift up. If this happens, pin-baste it down from behind temporarily, and, when the spirit moves you, iron the loose parts back down tightly. At inward points, that final three-thread-deep stitch at the "V" can be taken into the freezer paper.

PHOTO 8. "Wreath of Strawberry Leaves," Pattern #22. Appliqué and signature by Jean Stanclift; pattern drafting, fabric selection, and calligraphed inscription by Elly Sienkiewicz; 1988. (Photo: G. Staley)

BLOCK PREPARATION/PATTERN TRANSFER

Review the sections in "Part One: Getting Started" on freezer paper pattern transfer (Version II) and transferring patterns shown as a whole. Carefully fold your 12 1/2" square of freezer paper into fourths. Trace all four pages of the strawberry leaf wreath onto the freezer paper by quadrants. Cut the pattern out of the freezer paper except for the inner circle center. There, cut everything normally, but leave the dotted line area of the pattern attached to the wreath until after you've ironed the pattern onto the background.

PATTERN BRIDGES

Temporarily leaving the center of this pattern in place creates a "pattern bridge." These disposable bridges keep a fragile pattern from being ironed on crookedly to the appliqué fabric. This is a very useful concept which will be expanded upon in later lessons.

Heat-baste the wreath pattern, centered, onto the right side of your 16" square of green appliqué fabric. Once the pattern is positioned, carefully snip the dotted lines and pull out the pattern bridge center which has now served its purpose.

Flip the fabric over so that the paper pattern faces down. Iron the back of your fabric with firm, heavy pressure. Pay particular attention to points.

APPLIQUÉ METHOD—ONLAID CUTWORK WITH FREEZER PAPER ON TOP

To begin, pin-baste your two 16" squares of fabric together, right sides facing up. Move three small pins into the center of the wreath where you will start your "handle cut" (Lesson 1) beside an outward point. If you are left-handed, start sewing to the right of that point; if right-handed, start to the left.

Follow the cutwork appliqué method taught in Lesson 1. The appliqué technique is exactly the same except that now our turn line is marked by the freezer paper, rather than drawn. The one factor the "Wreath of Strawberry Leaves" pattern adds is the stems and leaves. When the fleur-de-lis of Lesson 1 had very little seam allowance to share between the right and left sides of a narrow inward point, we simply divided the difference equally and took a little more seam from each side if needed.

Now we want the stem to look like a stem, to be a continuous line leading into a leaf and then beyond it. This means that we'll take any extra seam allowance out of the leaf, not out of the stem. Luckily we'll get lots of practice on this pattern, for leaves and stems are the common denominator of Appliqué Album Quilts.

Use the tack stitch and progress from the inner circle of leaves to the outer. Begin the outer circle once again at an outward point. Our pattern is soothingly repetitious after the first few leaves. Thus, now is a good time to learn a new stitch.

Please meet a fine, upstanding traditional stitch which forms the very backbone of many accomplished appliquérs' repertoires. I give the blind stitch this unequivocal character reference to counterbalance its suspiciously long list of aliases. Think of them as nicknames born of affection. Their origins are revealed below.

THE BLIND STITCH
(Alias the Invisible Appliqué Stitch, the Ladder Stitch, the Pumpkin Stitch, the Jack-o'-Lantern Stitch, the Slip Stitch, the Speed Stitch, and the Hem Stitch)

The blind stitch is most useful on a straight edge or on gentle curves, as opposed to points or tight curves where the forceful little tack stitch performs best. Because the blind stitch can be "run," that is, several stitches on one needle and one pull-through of the thread, it can be much faster than the tack stitch. (Hence the names "slip stitch" and "speed stitch.") By the very nature of its process, 99% of blind stitches are hidden or invisible.

The blind stitch is easy to learn if you repeat its components to yourself as you sew. To memorize it, I broke the instructions into two phrases: "Into the green and out of the green. Into the white [background] and out of the white." Begin a few stitches into your travels along the gentle curve of the wreath circle (Figure 2-1).

1. Bring your needle up from behind, through the white fabric, right at the seam edge of the green (Figure 2-2).

2. Put the point of your needle into the green fold, move forward through the fold about 1/32", poke your needle out, and pull your thread through (Figure 2-3). That was "Into the green and out of the green."

3. Now, directly opposite where you exited the green, put your point straight down into the white. Repeat the same little straight stitch as in the green fold, but now it is into, under, and up out of the white. "Into the white and out of the white" (Figure 2-2, again).

4. Pull your thread through. So far this is no speed stitch, but just repeat to yourself, "A stitch in the green, a stitch in the white," until you've learned the serviceable blind stitch. Once you've learned it, you're ready to "run" your stitches together in speedy fashion.

About three stitches is what I'm comfortable getting on one pull-through of the needle. I end up pulling the thread through as my needle comes out of the green. The blind stitch soon becomes second nature.

Figure 2-4 shows clearly the path of thread in the blind stitch. You can see why it's also called the "Ladder Stitch." The "rungs" of the ladder run between the "stitch in the green, the stitch in the white." A more whimsical needlewoman recognized a pumpkin or Jack-o'-lantern's teeth in the pattern of the stitch. Perhaps she was up late one fine Halloween Eve, hemming a witch's cape when this vision materialized. For yes, the blind stitch is also the humble "hemming stitch" whose acquaintance you may have long since made.

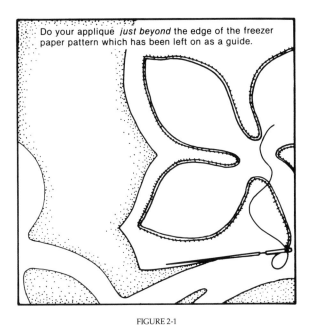

Do your appliqué *just beyond* the edge of the freezer paper pattern which has been left on as a guide.

FIGURE 2-1

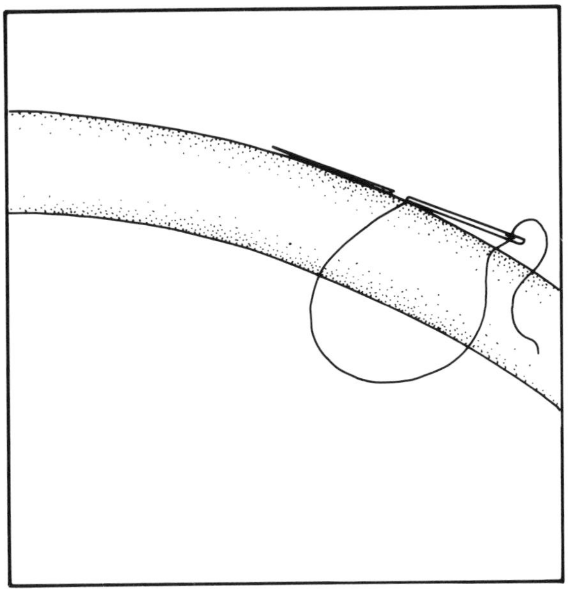

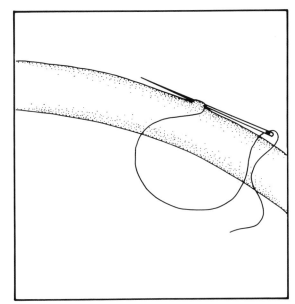

FIGURE 2-3

FIGURE 2-2

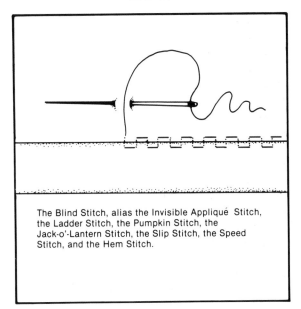

The Blind Stitch, alias the Invisible Appliqué Stitch, the Ladder Stitch, the Pumpkin Stitch, the Jack-o'-Lantern Stitch, the Slip Stitch, the Speed Stitch, and the Hem Stitch.

FIGURE 2-4

Our "Wreath of Strawberry Leaves" pattern has only short runs of gentle curves on leaf, wreath, and stem. You may decide that blind-stitching in only the 1 1/2" of gentle curve between acute angles takes too much concentration. In that case, tuck this new knowledge (or old friendship) away until Lesson 4. There, on a stellar block of the "Celestial Bodies" collection, you can string your stitches together along speedways of straight edges.

Another pattern to make using onlaid cutwork appliqué: "You Are Perfect," Pattern #3. This striking *scherenschnitte* block provides good practice on points, curves, and straight lines, and it's fairly easy to make.

NOTES

[1]Sienkiewicz, Elly, *Spoken Without a Word*.

LESSON 3:

Inlaid Cutwork Appliqué with Freezer Paper on Top, Appliqué in the Opposite Direction: Facing the Seam, a Smaller (1/8") Seam Allowance, and How to Do Inlaid Appliqué Without Freezer Paper, Plus Writing on Your Quilt

PATTERN:
"Love" or "Feather-Wreathed Heart with Doves," Pattern #13 (Photo 9)

Feather wreaths were favorite designs for inlaid ("reverse") appliqué in the mid-nineteenth century. This pattern will hone your inlaid appliqué skills to a master level. Appliquéing from the background fabric down to one color beneath it (rather than to several colors), and the curved nature of the pattern, typifies the inlaid appliqué of the classic Baltimore Album Quilts. As in Lesson 2, leaving the freezer paper pattern on as you sew adds a nontraditional modern convenience.

BLOCK PREPARATION/
PATTERN TRANSFER

Inlaid appliqué requires a negative freezer paper pattern. Cut the pattern for "Love" out of a 12 1/2" square of freezer paper. The square remains intact with the petaled shape of the heart and the two doves cut out from it. Review the section in "Part One: Getting Started" featuring Version II of freezer paper pattern transfer.

Iron your pattern onto your off-white background fabric. Cut a tiny slit through the off-white fabric in the very center of each "petal shape" in the wreath. Cut a small slit within each bird, beyond the 3/16" seam allowance. (Hint from Katherine Kuhn of Virginia: Cutting the slits before you baste your block together prevents the accidental piercing of your second layer.)

Pin-baste:
Lay your background fabric pattern side down on the table. Put your square of red appliqué fabric right side down on top of it. Pin-baste as before, with three additional pins in the area where you begin.

APPLIQUÉ METHOD—INLAID CUT-
WORK WITH FREEZER PAPER ON TOP

Inlaid appliqué is basically the same as onlaid appliqué in that you turn under a seam allowance

PHOTO 9. "Love," or "Feather-Wreathed Heart with Doves," Pattern #13. Appliqué by Gene Way; pattern drafting, fabric selection, tracing of George Bickham's eighteenth-century calligraphy and of Gene Way's signature by Elly Sienkiewicz; 1988. (Photo: G. Staley)

and sew the folded edge down. There are, however, three major differences between inlaid and onlaid appliqué:

1. The fabric order is reversed: the off-white is on top, the red is beneath. Thus the background fabric becomes the appliqué fabric, and the appliqué fabric becomes the background fabric.

2. Because of the reversed fabrics, the marking of the design is on the off-white and the appliqué thread is off-white.

   Can these factors help explain why inlaid appliqué was so popular a century and a half ago? In the pre-lightbox era, it would be easier to mark an exacting design like our feathered wreath, or a quilt's feathered border, by tracing it through (or onto) white fabric. At a time when 99% of all appliqué was done in pale (non-bleeding?) thread, the needlewomen would recognize the fact we all now depend upon: It is easier to hide stitches when the thread matches the appliqué fabric.

3. Tightly curved designs are easier to appliqué smoothly in inlaid appliqué than in onlaid appliqué. The simple reason for this is that the seam is turned under into a larger space in inlaid appliqué (Figure 3-1). In onlaid appliqué, the seam is being

squeezed back into a smaller space (Figure 3-2).

Perhaps just because mid-nineteenth-century needlewomen were so well-versed in all the modes of appliqué, they chose inlaid appliqué for patterns such as our feathered wreath because it is, in fact, the easiest way to do it.

To begin, review basic cutwork and the tack stitch, both discussed in Lesson 1. The cutwork appliqué

Inlaid Appliqué

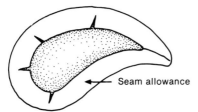

Seam allowance

Seam allowance is pushed back
into a larger area.

FIGURE 3-1

Onlaid Appliqué

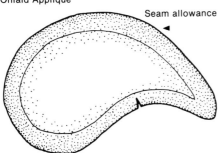

Seam allowance

Seam allowance is pushed back
into a smaller space.

FIGURE 3-2

Base of Petal

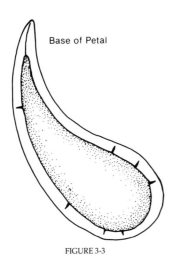

FIGURE 3-3

rules can be modified now that you are experienced and understand the principles. Rather than cutting just an inch or so at a time, cut a bit more where it makes sense. On this wreath, for example, cut out the whole inside of each "petal shape" when you are ready to sew it. It is appropriate now to use a smaller, 1/8" seam allowance which helps the curves turn under smoothly.

1. Begin by cutting the petal just to the right of the inside top center. Trim to a 1/8" seam beyond the paper pattern edge, inside the petal shape. Cut to one thread before the turn line, splitting the base of this petal (Figure 3-3).

2. On tight, concave curves, clip to two threads from the turn line, or as needed. Minimize clips—place them at the deepest parts of an inward curve. Sew to the immediate right and then the left of a clip so that it is smooth and tight.

3. Start your appliqué at the base of the petal. Needleturn the seam under. Tack-stitch to the left side if you're right-handed, to the right side if you're left-handed.

APPLIQUÉ IN THE OPPOSITE DIRECTION—FACING THE SEAM

After you've perfected these smooth, inward curves on a dozen petals or so, try something different. Let's start sewing from the petal base to the right, if you're right-handed, to the left, if you're left-handed.

You have been holding the block so that you face the appliqué—the seam you are sewing faces away from you. You look "over the seam" to sew (Figure 3-4A). Now, with the block turned around, you are facing the seam; the appliqué itself is away from you (Figure 3-4B). Practice this "appliqué in the opposite direction" for several petals.

Many people do all their appliqué facing the seam because you can see so clearly exactly what you are sewing (Figure 3-5). My preference is to hold the appliqué toward my body, the seam facing away as we started in Lesson 1. This is because I love cutwork appliqué and find needleturning under by pulling towards me, especially on points, much easier than pushing the seam under away from me.

In the interest of staying flex   though, I try to find occasion to appliqué in the opposite direction. To me it feels most comfortable in basted

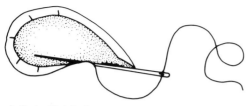

A. Tack stitch facing
the appliqué.

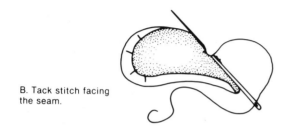

B. Tack stitch facing
the seam.

FIGURES 3-4A & 3-4B

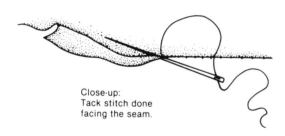

Close-up:
Tack stitch done
facing the seam.

FIGURE 3-5

appliqué methods where the seam is already turned under and basted in place (Lesson 10). There you don't depend so heavily on your thumb preparing and fingerpressing the seams out ahead of your sewing needle.

After finishing the wreath's inside, reverse appliqué the doves while the bulk of the fabric is still holding them in place. Next return to complete the outer petals of the feathered heart.

As you sew, savor the pleasure of this rhythmic appliqué pattern. It lets you become so familiar with it that you can practice the tack stitch, the blind stitch, the seam towards you, the seam away. Find for yourself which works best on this appliqué task, and give yourself credit for having remained flexible.

To do inlaid appliqué without freezer paper, simply draw around the pattern, marking your turn line onto your off-white fabric. You may want to simply trace one vertical half of the pattern from

the two book pages, and transfer it to your fabric by dressmaker's carbon paper. (See "Part One: Getting Started" for details on the two-page pattern transfer method.)

Without the freezer paper to hold the pattern flat, baste all around the pattern, 1/4" inside the appliqué as you did the center of the fleur-de-lis in Lesson 1 (Figure 1-16). This prevents any distortion.

WRITING ON YOUR QUILT

Our pattern has an ornate calligraphy word "Love" penned exuberantly in its center. Whatever you choose to write in the center, the method is simple:

1. Carefully write the words out on paper first. Fit them, centered, to the space allotted.

2. See the section in "Part One: Getting Started" on "Other Supplies and Equipment" for a discussion of pens. Test the pen and your strokes on scrap fabric. You want to get the feel of "drawing" the words, rather than writing them. You will want to find just the right speed and pressure so that the pen does not blotch the fabric.

3. Stabilize your background fabric. This can be done by ironing freezer paper to the underneath side or by stiffening the fabric with spray starch. I prefer to use the starch, because the freezer paper adds one more layer to see through over a lightbox. If you decide to use the starch, spray and iron from the back side of the fabric. The Magic Sizing™ spray starch that I use seems to have the added advantage of helping to prevent the ink from bleeding.

4. Work on a lightbox. Center the words under your background fabric. Pin the paper to this fabric so that it cannot shift.

5. Trace the writing onto the fabric. On something as fancy as "Love," I turn the lightbox off periodically to see where I am and to do some filling in of thicker strokes. Iron to set.

Another pattern to make using inlaid cutwork: "Feather-Wreathed Heart," Pattern #14. Pure elegance!

LESSON 4:

Celestial Bodies: Masterpiece Straight-edge Appliqué, Plus Sharper Points

PATTERN:
"Divine Guidance I" (Eight- and Twelve-Pointed Stars), Pattern #4 (Photo 10)

The mid-nineteenth century was the heyday of appliqué. And nothing shows this more surely than the existence of those patterns which before and after this period were *tours de force* of precision piecing, but which during this time were taken up as the Appliqué Challenge. That the challenge was well met is evidenced by constellations of appliquéd Stars, Mariner's Compasses, border upon border in appliquéd triangles, and even appliquéd log-cabin-step-type patterns.

"Divine Guidance I" provides nice long runs of several straight-edged inches on which to practice. You'll be ready for those challenging eight-pointed stars in the corners by the time you've worked your way out to them. If you love appliquéing these stars, go on to make the magnificent nineteenth-century "Feathered Star" (Pattern #5, from "Sarah McIlwain's Quilt").[1] From thenceforth, entire constellations are at your fingertips!

BLOCK PREPARATION/
PATTERN TRANSFER

1. Fold a 12 1/2" square of freezer paper into precise quarters. Open up the paper and very carefully trace Pattern #4 onto the uppermost quarter of the square. Trace the dotted pattern bridges (Lesson 2). Use a small, grided see-through ruler to keep the lines precise. When you refold your square, remember to staple the stars to keep the layers from shifting as you cut the template.

2. Cut the pattern out as one piece. Pierce the inlaid appliqué portions of the pattern with your sharp tailor-point scissors and cut out the centers. Be very careful to keep all points attached (Figure 4-1). This will help remind you that they remain attached and out of one piece of cloth in the appliqué process. Remove the staples and open up the pattern.

PHOTO 10. "Divine Guidance I," Pattern #4. Appliqué by Mary Anne Johnson; pattern drafting and fabric selection by Elly Sienkiewicz; 1988. (Photo: D. Sienkiewicz)

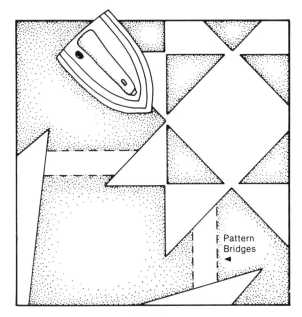

FIGURE 4-1

Review "Part One: Getting Started" for details of the pattern transfer method (Version II). On a hard surface, iron this pattern down tightly. Returning to the right side, give every point a firm jab with the point of the iron.

1. Center your pattern on the right side of the top appliqué fabric. Heat baste in place (Figure 4-1, also). Iron the four corner stars down lightly. Once they are affixed in place, carefully cut off the pattern bridges.

Their job of positioning these separate design elements is now completed. Flip your fabric over, pattern side down and iron.

2. Pin-baste the top and background fabrics together from behind as previously. Pin-baste the center where you will start with three additional pins from behind.

APPLIQUÉ METHOD—ONE-COLOR INLAID AND ONLAID CUTWORK APPLIQUÉ WITH FREEZER PAPER ON TOP

The method for doing straight-edged appliqué is basically the same as the "freezer paper on top" method for inlaid and onlaid appliqué taught in Lessons 2 and 3. Review those lessons again briefly.

I hope, like me, you are quite in love with this method. If you are not yet convinced of its virtues, give it one more chance. The straight-cut edge of the freezer paper provides a clear, exact turn line. The appliqué fabric is kept flat and aligned. This allows you easily to appliqué the kind of precise, straight lines which 99% of our contemporaries would approach by piecing.

Begin on one of the center inlaid triangles. Cut to 1/8" from the seam, then needleturn the seam under and appliqué as in Lesson 3. Next, start one of the large star's outer points. (Right-handers sew to the left of the point, left-handers to the right.) Make a long-handled cut to the point as described in Lesson 1, then appliqué. At inner and outer points, use the sturdy, strong tack stitch. On those long straight runs, use the quick blind stitch to make good time.

Smaller seam allowances:
Because this pattern has fine sharp points, use a 1/8" seam allowance to diminish their bulk. By looking at Lee Porter's 1846-47 Baltimore Album Quilt on a lightbox, I was able to see that a 1/8" to 1/16" seam was the size most commonly used. No pattern markings of any kind were visible. This tiny seam must simply have been needleturned under "by eye."

Your seams will be similarly tiny in the corners of the inlaid portions of the design. You may be eyeing those eight-pointed stars now and think-

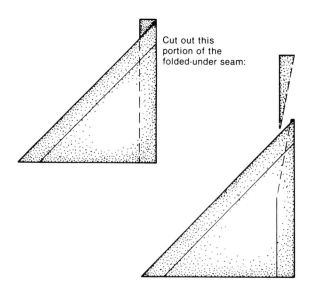

Cut out this portion of the folded-under seam:

FIGURE 4-2

ing to yourself that you will surely need divine guidance in those spots. Fear not, if you are slow and sure, you'll turn the corners nicely. The secret to such narrow connections between points is to shove the seam allowance back hard against the opposite side which is already sewn down. You then firmly tack-stitch the seam in place.

"Paper-doilies":
If you can do the little stars, you can literally do any cutwork pattern, antique or new. This includes those lacy paper-doily-like *scherenschnitte* cutwork patterns in the classic quilts. Having attained the skill to do such ornate blocks is quite an accomplishment. Congratulations!

Sharper points:
Bernice Enyeart gave me a hint for how to cut bulk out of sharp points having larger seam allowances. She attributed this trick to Nancy Pearson. When extra fabric must be cut out, lift the appliqué's unsewn edge up, reach under it with your fine scissors, and take a triangular snip off the right-hand seam which has already been sewn down. Because it is already very tightly sewn down, it won't fray the way a cut close across the unsewn top of the point would (Figure 4-2).

Bernice also attributed another clever method to Nancy that you should practice on these star points. To give a point the appearance of being very sharp, go back after you've locked the point and take a slightly longer, visible stitch straight out from the point. With thread carefully matched, this gives the illusion of a very sharp appliquéd point. Both Bernice and Nancy are world-class appliquérs, so I took their advice to heart.

MORE ABOUT STRAIGHT-EDGE APPLIQUÉ AND STARS

My first clue that yesteryear's appliqué passion extended even to appliquéing patterns which had traditionally been pieced came at a show of nineteenth-century quilts. I was enjoying a sharpness of vision made possible by my new magnifying half-glasses. "Appliqué quilt with pieced border," read the museum catalog. Pieced?

I leaned across the guard rope and held my glasses at arm's length. My effort was rewarded, as I was able to see firsthand that this dogtooth (isosceles triangle) border was not pieced, but appliquéd from a long strip of fabric. Moreover, as I would from then on observe repeatedly, the appliqué was finely done in white thread.

Dogtooth borders:

"Dogtooth" is the nineteenth-century English name for this border as noted by Averil Colby in her book, *Patchwork*. Unlike the "sawtooth" or right-angle borders, the isosceles dogtooth border adapts marvelously to appliqué. Its almost magically easy construction is covered in *Baltimore Beauties, Volume II*, in the chapter on borders.

The dogtooth border was exceptionally popular during this Victorian period. You can see a unique example in quilt #1. The Star of Bethlehem in the center is pieced, while its double borders are clearly appliquéd.

But why a star in the center of a classic period Baltimore Quilt? Stars actually abound in these quilts. In the Baltimore Museum of Art's exhibition catalog, 12 out of the 24 quilts have stars. Within these 12, there are over 30 stars either depicted as such or formed by other appliqué motifs within a block.

The suspicion grew on me that some of these stars might well be appliquéd rather than pieced. A trip to Sotheby's in New York City provided the needed closer look. Eureka! In "Sarah McIlwain's Album Quilt," a striking Turkey-red feathered-star block was appliquéd from one piece of cloth. Looking back now through the Baltimore Museum of Art catalog with this insight, one can see other stars which are appliquéd as well.

The answer to "Why so many stars?" probably lies in the star's symbolic meaning of "divine guidance." A wish for divine guidance would seem an appropriate and enriching inclusion in any Presentation Quilt. We see stars as prominently displayed as the medallion center of Baltimore quilt #1 (see the Color Section) and as the medallion border of Beyond Baltimore quilt #5. In some very ornate Baltimore Album Quilts (quilt #2, block D-2, for example), stars are formed by floral medallions within wreaths. This is, I suppose, because these blended better with this ornate, florid aesthetic style than did the bare straight lines of traditionally depicted stars.

Stars with from five to sixteen points appear in the Baltimore Museum catalog's collection of Album Quilts. These stars include the full range of star symbolism in Christian iconography. Beyond divine guidance, other symbolic meanings for stars are given in this book in "Part Four: The Patterns." Additional star meanings which seem intended in these classic quilts are the "Eastern Star" (five points, set on point) of the Masons and the "Lone Star" of Texas. Masonic and Odd Fellow symbols recur in these quilts. So do references to "Texas" and heroes of the Mexican-American War. Undoubtedly the desire to try one's hand at the challenge of appliquéing a "pieced" star also contributed to the prevalence of stars.

Other celestial patterns to make: "Divine Guidance II" (this is essentially the same pattern as Pattern #4, but in two colors); "Feathered Star," Pattern #5; and "Star of Hearts," Pattern #6.

NOTES

[1]Sienkiewicz, Elly, "My Baltimore Album Quilt Discoveries," *Quilter's Newsletter Magazine*, #202, pp. 26-27.

LESSON 5:

Adding a Second Color—Unit Cutwork Appliqué; Patterns Adapted for Cutwork; Cutwork Islands; Layering, Abutting, Needleturn, and Pattern-bridged Islands for Cutwork; and Placing Appliqués on Grain

PATTERNS:

"Crossed Laurel Sprays," Pattern #7 (Photo 11); "$200,000 Tulips," Pattern #8 (Photo 12); and "Hospitality," Pattern #9 (Photo 13)

The advantages of cutwork appliqué are many. But can you use cutwork on multicolor blocks as well? Happily, the answer is yes. You can use cutwork on any block where one color unit predominates and can be appliquéd down first. Most of those red and green blocks in vogue during the classic Baltimore Album Quilt period are therefore appropriate for unit cutwork.

Less commonly, you may find a pattern equally divided between two colors. In this case, pick the most sensible one to apply first. I stipulate "any color which can be laid down first" because it seems to me too hard to try to properly line up a large marked piece of fabric over a background block which has elements already appliquéd to it. And after all, our object is ease as well as efficiency.

PATTERNS ADAPTED FOR CUTWORK

Our "Crossed Laurel Sprays" pattern (Photo 11) is drafted especially for cutwork. This means that the leaves are *attached* to the stem rather than being separate units which abut it or go under it. You will develop an eye for which blocks can easily be done by cutwork and a sense for how to adapt your patterns for it.

Well-drafted, finely-sewn cutwork is recognizably different from the same design done as individual shapes. For an example of this, see the two "Fleur-de-Lis and Folded Rosebuds" appliqués pictured in the Lesson Blocks in the Color Section. Using the pattern in *Spoken Without a Word*, Daphne Hedges made Version I by separate unit appliqué with inlaid rosebuds (see Color Plate #19 in the Color Section). My block,

PHOTO 11. "Crossed Laurel Sprays," Pattern #7. Appliqué, pattern drafting, fabric selection, and calligraphed signature by Elly Sienkiewicz, 1985; quilting by Virginia Lemasters, 1988. (Photo: G. Staley)

Version II, has been adapted for unit cutwork (Color Plate #18). The hallmarks of this adaptation are that the leaves and calyxes remain *attached* to the stem. It is interesting to note that, when seen from the distance of photographs, many classic versions of this block also appear to have been cut and sewn from one attached piece of cloth. The addition of my folded rosebuds is in keeping with the Victorian fondness for three-dimensional flowers.

Economy/precision trade-off:

I was given a wonderful primitive mid-nineteenth-century block quilt of Crossed Laurel Sprays. The diagonals of the sprays (stems with attached leaves) are each a separate fabric unit. Crossing two separate strips of fabric lacks the alignment precision of making an "X" of the sprays from a whole square of cloth. These crossed sprays all a-tilt give a delightful folk art look to the quilt. Using a strip of fabric for each diagonal, as on these antique blocks, is undeniably more economical than cutting the whole "X" out of one piece of green as I have done for our Lesson Block. But that is the trade-off: economy for easy precision.

Here precision is chosen. The green unit cutwork pattern is marked on a whole square of fabric. Now that you are thoroughly familiar with cutwork block preparation, you can economize on the appliqué fabric. As a rule of thumb, the cutwork appliqué fabric square need only be 1/2" bigger on each side than the appliqué's outside edges. In this case, that would be about a 13 1/2" square of green.

FABRIC CHOICE

My block uses a solid green and red. This type of block in the Baltimore Album Quilt period is more likely to have been done in a green print. It was often a dark leaf-green with a small black geometric print on it. Sometimes our needlesisters of yore added variety and softened the black by using this print wrong-side up, as well as right-side up. Turkey red seems to be the color most commonly found as a solid, though Turkey red calicoes abound in these quilts as well.

BLOCK PREPARATION/ PATTERN TRANSFER

See "Part One: Getting Started" for details. Iron the freezer paper pattern for the green leaf/stem unit, centered, onto the green fabric. Match the diagonals of both your background and green fabrics for easy centering of the 13 1/2" green square on the 16" background block (Figure 5-1). Pin-baste.

APPLIQUÉ METHOD—UNIT CUTWORK

1. Begin atop a stem. (You will leave its tip raw in the end.) If you are right-handed, start moving down the left stem side; if left-handed, start down the right (see Figure 5-2).

2. At the leaf juncture, take any added seam needed out of the leaf, not out of the stem, which needs to remain straight (Figure 5-3A).

3. When you come around the leaf to the other side of this joint, you will simply shove your seam allowance under tightly against the side which is already sewn down. Tack this fabric into its cramped resting place with secure, well-tugged stitches (Figure 5-3B).

Cutwork islands:
Once fully around the block, you are ready to make "cutwork islands." These are small separate appliqué motifs treated temporarily as one unit; they are marked on *one* piece of cloth to be applied by cutwork. The cutwork island units here are the sets of three close red leaves which crown each stem. These three-leaf units create an opportunity to perform an interesting experiment.

The hypothesis is this: "Appliqués should be cut on the same grain as the background cloth

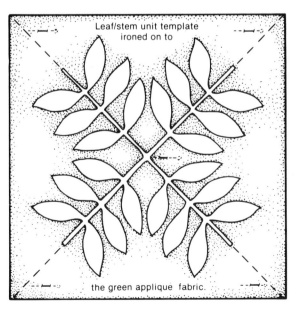

FIGURE 5-1

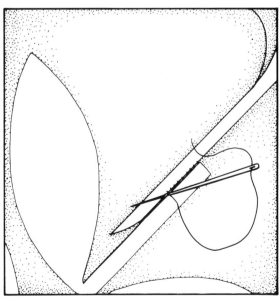

FIGURE 5-2

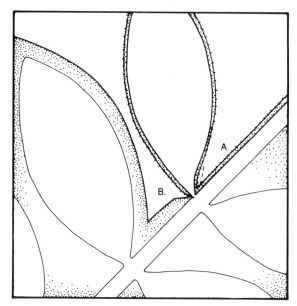

FIGURES 5-3A & 5-3B

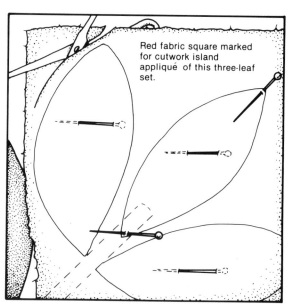

FIGURE 5-5

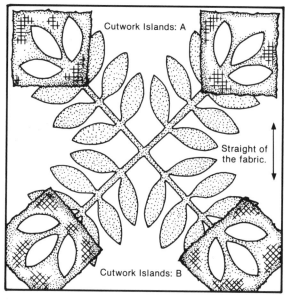

FIGURES 5-4A & 5-4B

The results of your experiment will be apparent when your appliqué is finished. The question is: Are the red leaf units on opposite ends of the block, two on-grain, two off-grain, noticeably different from each other at normal range?

3. Again, working on your lightbox, pin one red leaf-set over the end of a laurel spray. Pin the top and bottom of the middle red leaf in place over the stem (Figure 5-5). Since the three leaves were traced as one unit, placing the center one means that those on either side of it fall naturally into place.

4. Pin-baste behind each leaf. This way you won't set any leaf "adrift" as you progress by cutwork appliqué from one side of this unit to the other (Figure 5-5, also).

By approaching these red leaves as one cutwork island, you benefit from ease of pattern transfer, perfect pattern alignment, and speed in getting started—all advantages of whole-block cutwork. Make the four center red leaves into one cutwork island as well.

ADDING A SECOND COLOR AS INDIVIDUAL APPLIQUÉ MOTIFS— THE "$200,000 TULIPS" PATTERN

Once you've mastered the "Crossed Laurel Sprays" pattern, a charming design to move on to is the $200,000 Tulips block (Photo 12). Here, as is

they'll rest on. They will look better on the same grain, and will lie flatter. Moreover, they *should* be done this way." To test this hypothesis:

1. Working on your lightbox, trace two of the red leaf-sets *on-grain* (Figure 5-4A). Pin them squarely to the sprays at the top of the block. Thus they will be on the same grain as both the background and the green leaf/stem unit.

2. Next trace two of the red leaf-sets *off-grain* by laying the fabric askew on the pattern (Figure 5-4B). You will sew both these leaf-units to the sprays at the bottom of the block.

PHOTO 12. "$200,000 Tulips," Pattern #8. Appliqué by Jane Doak; pattern drafting, fabric selection, and Jane Doak's calligraphed signature by Elly Sienkiewicz; 1988. (Photo: G. Staley)

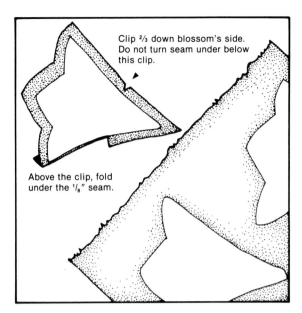

Clip ²/₃ down blossom's side. Do not turn seam under below this clip.

Above the clip, fold under the ¹/₈" seam.

FIGURE 5-7

Leave the seam open on the blossom side of the calyxes.

FIGURE 5-6

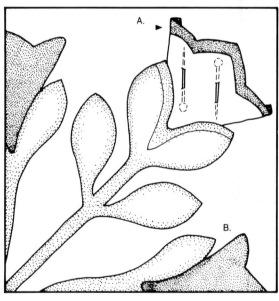

A.

B.

FIGURES 5-8A & 5-8B

most often the case, the second color has to be added as *individual units* rather than as an island of several motifs. Briefly, here's the process:

1. The green stem/leaf/vase unit is approached by the unit cutwork method. Appliqué all the green except the blossom side of the calyxes which you leave open (Figure 5-6).

2. Next, iron the freezer paper tulip patterns onto the right side of the red fabric and trim the seam to 1/8" to 1/16". (Warning: If a fabric is loosely woven, you must leave a

3/16" seam.) Clip the seam two-thirds down on either side. Fold the seams under above the clips (Figure 5-7).

3. The freezer paper provides just enough stiffness to slip the bloom under the open calyx. Pin-baste with two pins so that this tiny unit doesn't shift. Small units are deceptively mobile (Figure 5-8A).

4. Appliqué the outside rim of the tulip, leaving the part tucked under the calyx flat and unseamed.

5. Needleturn under the green calyx's seam. Appliqué this folded edge over the flat tulip edge, completing the flower (Figure 5-8B).

6. Iron the freezer paper pattern onto your red fabric for the last motif, the crown of hearts which decorates the tulip vases. Trim the seam. Pin-baste and apply this unit by "needleturn appliqué." Transfer the pattern with temporary bridges, then leave the freezer paper pattern on top to keep the shape precise (Figure 5-9).

NEEDLETURN APPLIQUÉ

Needleturn appliqué is simply the name for what we have been doing since Lesson 1. That is, turning under the seam with our needle as we go along, then appliquéing down this folded edge.

In this lesson, we are separating the process of "needleturn appliqué" where the whole unit is cut out before you sew, from that of "cutwork appliqué" where no cutting is done until you are ready to sew (or to "needleturn").

In needleturn appliqué, as in cutwork appliqué, you can a) leave a freezer paper pattern on top, or b) simply have your units marked with a drawn line, or c) go one step further and just cut the shape out and needleturn by eye. Needleturn is thus the most basic appliqué model, like the Model-T Ford. For an example of incredibly fine appliqué done by needleturn alone, see Donna Collins' Miniature Baltimore Medallion Quilt (Color Plate #17).

All evidence I've seen points to even the fanciest Baltimore Album Quilts having been done this no-frills way. Thus our basic, serviceable needleturn appliqué, like the Model T, takes you anyplace you want to go!

The romantic name "island cutwork" and talk of needleturning bring up an interesting question. If cutwork is so wonderful, why isn't it used in Hawaiian quiltmaking? Elizabeth Akana, noted Hawaiian quilt authority, suggested to me that the threat of rust from pin-basting could, by itself, keep this method out of the nineteenth-century tropical quiltmaker's repertoire.

Lots of other possibilities occur to me, though. Foremost is the fact that Hawaiian appliqués are cut directly from the folded cloth. This pattern transfer method seems to have been a style in the nineteenth century on the mainland (and in England, according to Averil Colby). However, if I were now making a whole-quilt appliqué, I would surely safety-pin-baste. Then I would "cut

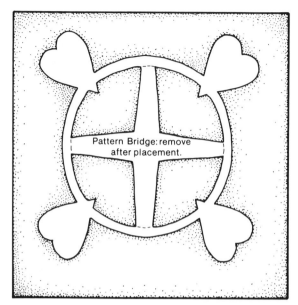

FIGURE 5-9

PHOTO 13. "Hospitality," Pattern #9. Appliqué by Joanne Turnley; pattern drafting and fabric selection by Elly Sienkiewicz; 1988. (Photo: G. Staley)

and sew, cut and sew," as Charlotte Patera advised.

CUTWORK ISLANDS CREATED BY PATTERN BRIDGES

Sometimes you must add pattern bridges (Lesson 2) to get the benefit of unit cutwork. In the two-color pineapple block, Hospitality (Photo 13), the red makes a natural whole unit for cutwork. But clearly there are eight separate green units which must go on first, to lie under the red. Moreover, appliquéing down the straight, narrow pineapple

FIGURE 5-10

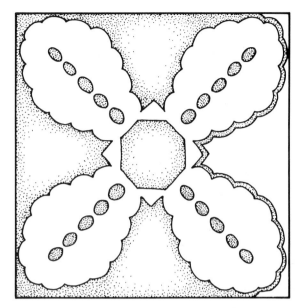

FIGURE 5-12

FIGURE 5-11

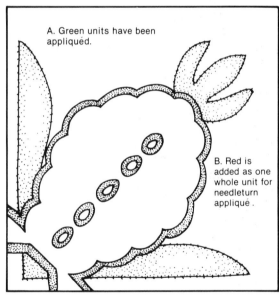

FIGURE 5-13

leaves parallel and true would take painstaking care by other methods.

The solution is seen in Figure 5-10. Temporary pattern bridges join disparate elements into cutwork islands for the benefits of cutwork placement. The bridges are then cut off and discarded, so that the cut and sew method can be used (Figure 5-11). The placement is perfect.

Because the green had to be appliquéd down first, you must trim back to the 1/8" seam allowance on the red "pineapple" section of the pattern so that you can see where it goes (Figures 5-12 and 5-13).

"LAYERING" VERSUS "ABUTTING"

In our red/green Lesson Blocks, we've placed an appliqué motif over or under another motif. Our red leaves went over our stems. Our red tulips went under their calyxes. This is called layering and common sense tells us when and how to do it. Leaves traditionally grow out from under the larger stem motif but are placed on top of tiny stem ends. Flowers traditionally grow out from under their calyxes, but are placed on top of stems.

Abutting is the opposite of layering. In this, the seams of two contiguous appliqués are turned under within themselves. This gives you flexibility: you don't have to pre-think a pattern. It can also give you bulk and joints which aren't quite continuous. Unless you have a clear reason to abut, you are much more likely to get a smooth, pleasing result by layering than by abutting. If you are creating as you sew, or find that you want to fill a gap by abutting a leaf, then by all means do it. In a hundred years, if someone looks closely enough to notice the abutment, she may say, "Look! This is original: she was designing as she went. This might be a prototype block on which so many similar ones were based. How exciting!"

Posterity will look favorably on whatever we make, if only because it is old. We should be as gentle with each other and with ourselves. At least be practical. If you have to abut, do it. If your appliqué will look better layered, do it.

One final thought on layering vs. abutting: All these options form your creative tools. Don't lose a tool because someone else tells you not to use it. Sometimes, as I did on leaves in the "Ruched Rose Lyre" (Lesson 8), you may want to abut to emphasize the repeated separateness of each shape. Or you may want to do it for your own reasons. Have the courage of your convictions. We will all benefit more by you following your inner star, if it leads you in a different direction, than by your being hemmed in by too many do's and don'ts.

THE SAME GRAIN QUESTION

"Should appliqués be placed on the same grain as the background fabric?" I made the experiment on the red laurel leaves which has been suggested above. The block I did it on is one of this lesson's sample blocks, Crossed Laurel Sprays. I could tell you my results, but wouldn't you rather see your own "in the cloth"?

Close scrutiny of dozens of classic Baltimore Album Quilts reveals no predominance of appliqués placed on-grain. In fact, those good Ladies of Baltimore seem ignorant of the "on-grain" rule, or disregardful of it. Their quilts are beautiful, have lasted well, and have more than held their value.

The same-grain rule makes sense to me only on large appliqués. The cutwork placement method automatically aligns grains, so all of our larger block motifs from previous lessons are on-grain. The question: "How large must an appliqué be before it should be placed on-grain?" needs to be investigated. Perhaps one of you will begin this research with your red leaf experiment. I hope you'll share your results.

LESSON 6:

Unit Cutwork with Folded Fabric Flowers, Rectangle Roses, and Circle Roses, Plus Stitched Rose Hairs

PATTERNS:

"Fleur-de-Lis with Folded Rosebuds II," Pattern #10 (Photo 14), and "Sweetheart Rose Lyre," Pattern #15 (Photo 15)

The three-dimensional look was clearly highly prized in the classic Baltimore Album Quilts. Stuffed appliqué (Lesson 7) was common in these quilts and is sometimes quite amazing to our eye. Such exuberantly stuffed fruit can be seen in the circa 1845 epergne block in Photo 16. Contemporary quiltmakers have rediscovered lost three-dimensional folded fabric techniques[1] such as ruching which is described in Lesson 8. And we have added our own, such as my two folded rosebud versions. They are easy, charming, and seem to add another dimension of beauty.

BLOCK PREPARATION/ PATTERN TRANSFER

See "Part One: Getting Started" for details on transfering patterns shown at one-quarter block for "Fleur-de-Lis with Folded Rosebuds II," and patterns shown at one-half of the block for "Sweetheart Rose Lyre." Pin-baste for cutwork.

APPLIQUÉ METHOD— UNIT CUTWORK

In both patterns, the green leaf-and-stem fabric is the one appliquéd down first by unit cutwork. You are now well versed in this from Lesson 5.

FLEUR-DE-LIS WITH FOLDED ROSEBUDS II

1. Begin by sewing the complete green wreath-leaf section by unit cutwork appliqué (Lesson 5). Here again, where additional seam allowance is needed it must come out of the *underside* of the leaf, not out of the wreath.
    Leave the rosebud calyxes unsewn on the *bud side* so that the folded rosebuds can be slipped under them later. Leave the

PHOTO 14. "Fleur-de-Lis with Folded Rosebuds II," Pattern #10. Appliqué, pattern drafting, fabric selection, and signature by Elly Sienkiewicz, 1985; quilting by Carol White, 1986. This is block A-3 in quilt #6, shown in the Color Section. (Photo: © G. E. Garrison 1988)

PHOTO 15. "Sweetheart Rose Lyre," Pattern #15. Appliqué, pattern drafting, fabric selection, embroidery, and calligraphed signature by Elly Sienkiewicz, 1988. (Photo: G. Staley)

wreath's corners unsewn to layer the fleur-de-lis under the wreath stem.

2. Add the fleur-de-lis next. Appliqué these as separate motifs by needleturn with the freezer paper pattern left on top (Lesson 5). When your four fleurs-de-lis are completed, make the folded fabric roses.

PHOTO 16. A somewhat primitive Victorian epergne of fruit depicted in a theorem-style balance. This is a delightful example of the Baltimore quiltmakers' fondness for stuffed appliqué with its cannonball-like grapes and the heavily ridged melons. From a "circa 1845 Baltimore Album Quilt made by a member of the LeCompte family." (Photo: The Baltimore Museum of Art: Gift of Mr. and Mrs. H. Lloyd LeCompte, Jr., Baltimore. BMA 1976.98.8)

Method I: Folded fabric roses from a rectangle of fabric:

Cut eight 3" x 5" rectangles of red fabric for the medium and large rosebuds on either side of the center sides of the wreath.

Cut four 2" x 3" rectangles of red for the small inner corner rosebuds. Note: A satin ribbon could be used instead.

1. Fold the top inch of the rectangle to the wrong side of the fabric, folding lengthwise along the 5" side (Figure 6-1A).

2. From the center of the long edge, fold the left side down at a right angle (Figure 6-1B).

3. From a point 1/4" to the right of the center, fold the right side down to run 1/4" parallel to the left-hand fold (Figure 6-1C).

4. From a point 1" down the left-hand edge, fold from left to right at an angle (Figure 6-1D).

5. From a point 1" down the right-hand edge, fold from right to left at an angle. Here you

are folding under a lot of fabric. You can carefully cut out a bit from the top layer of the left-hand fold. Or, at least the first time, just pull the left-hand fold excess down a bit, out of the way of the right-hand fold (Figure 6-1E).

6. Put a pin through the folded layers, 1/4" below where they cross (Figure 6-1F).

7. Now pin through the dot on the calyx, on your paper pattern, to test whether your rose nicely fills the space of the rose drawn there (Figure 6-1G). The lower folds of the rose should show just above the calyx's seam turn line. Tack-stitch the rose where the pin was, to hold all layers together.

8. Work on your lightbox. Lay your background cloth on top of the pattern. Place a pin to mark your background cloth where the tip of each of the 12 rosebuds comes. This mark is important to show you how far down into the calyx you must push each folded rose.

9. Using your pattern as a guide, cut the bottom of the rose to fit into and fill the calyx.

10. Slip a rose into a calyx on the outside of the wreath. Push it down with your scissors until the top of the rosebud comes to the marking pin. Pin the rosebud in place securely (Figure 6-1H).

11. Appliqué the calyx down over the rose. Sew through the top layer of the rose only (Figure 6-1I). Tack the outer edge of the rose down (to prevent "wilt"), but leave its inner folds intriguingly free.

The above directions make the four medium-size roses around the outer edge of the wreath. To make the four larger roses inside the wreath, follow the same steps, but simply change the measurements:

On Step 3, move 1/3" to the right to fold down right to left, 1/3" parallel to the left-hand fold (Figure 6-1C, also).

On Step 4, move 1 1/3" down the left-hand edge to start your fold from left to right. Similarly on Step 5, move down 1 1/3" to start the fold (Figures 6-1C and 6-1D).

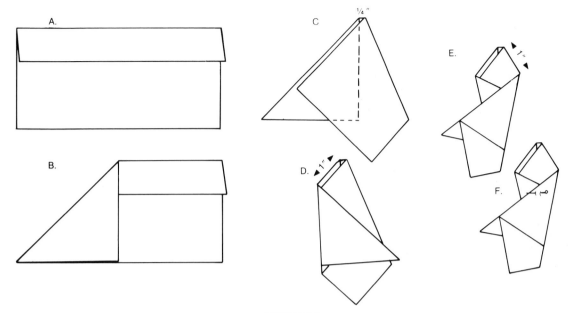

A.

B.

C.

¼ "

D. ◀ 1"▶

E. ◀ 1"▶

F.

FIGURE 6-1 A-F

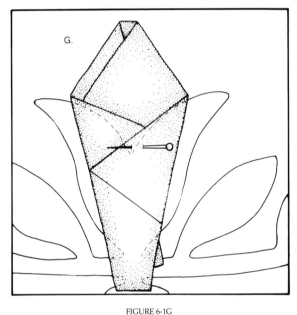

G.

FIGURE 6-1G

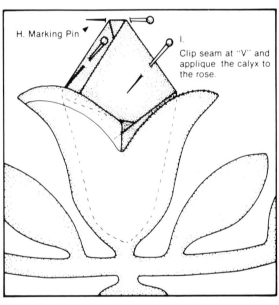

H. Marking Pin ▶

I.

Clip seam at "V" and applique the calyx to the rose.

FIGURES 6-1H & 6-1I

**To make the baby rosebuds
in each of the corners:**

1. Follow Steps 1 through 3 above. The only difference is that you are using a 2" x 3" rectangle, so you will be folding the long edge down one-third of the rectangle's 2" width in Step 1.

2. After following Steps 1 through 3, put a large quilting thread spool at the tip of the rosebud, and draw the circle portion on the folded fabric (Figure 6-2A).

3. Sew running stitches 1/4" inside (bud base side) this line and trim fabric off below the stitches (Figure 6-2B).

4. Tug to gather just enough to fit the corner calyx perfectly. Pin in place. Finish with Steps 10 and 11 above.

THE SWEETHEART ROSE LYRE

I am in love with this block! It is constructed using unit cutwork appliqué, following the same in-

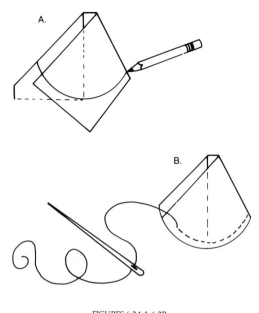

FIGURES 6-2A & 6-2B

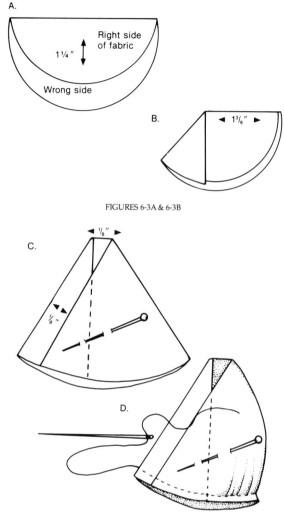

FIGURES 6-3A & 6-3B

FIGURES 6-3C & 6-3D

structions as for the "Fleur-de-Lis and Folded Rosebuds II" unit appliqué method given at the beginning of this lesson.

The one difference in this pattern is that the calyx has elegant spidery "fingers" that clutch the rose (Figure 6-4). To make these, trim 3/16" across the top of all three "fingers," treating them as one unit. Don't cut between them until you have inserted the rose. This way they aren't fragile and you can blissfully shove the blossom down atop a scissors (Figure 6-3E). Once the basted rose is pinned in place, cut between the calyx fingers and tightly appliqué them over the rose (Figure 6-3F).

Method II: Folded fabric roses from fabric circles:

1. Cut sixteen 3" diameter circles (pattern provided). Though it is easiest to use cotton fabric, which is stiffer than silk, I used exquisite, hand-painted silk by Maria Mc-Cormick Snyder for my roses. Mark the silk, which is slippery, using a window template. Make your own or buy an architectural circle template from an art supply store.

2. Fold the top 1 1/4" of the circle down over the wrong side of the fabric (Figure 6-3A).

3. Begin the next fold 1 3/8" in from the right edge of the circle. Fold the circle's left edge down at a right angle (Figure 6-3B).

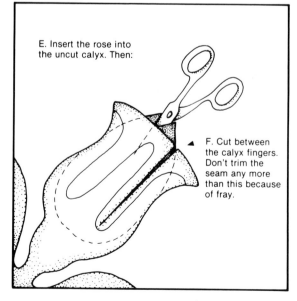

E. Insert the rose into the uncut calyx. Then:

F. Cut between the calyx fingers. Don't trim the seam any more than this because of fray.

FIGURES 6-3E & 6-3F

4. Starting about 1/8" to the right of this last fold, fold the right side down at an angle so that it runs 1/8" parallel to the left-hand fold. Pin at the base of the folds' overlap (Figure 6-3C).

5. Make a running stitch just inside the half circle. Tug gently, and watch the rose gather ever so slightly into a "Sweetheart" of a rose (Figure 6-3D). Eye your pattern to see about how full this rose should be. Tack-stitch to lock your gathering stitches. The bud will flatten and fold inside its calyx.

6. Insert the rose into its uncut calyx (Figure 6-3E). Pin it in place.

7. Cut carefully between the calyx fingers and appliqué them over the rose (Figure 6-3F). Tack-stitch down the rose's outer edge.

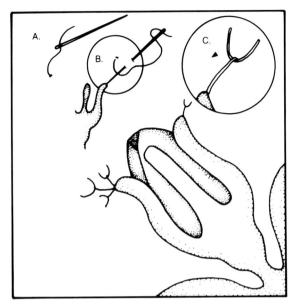

FIGURES 6-4A, 6-4B, & 6-4C

EMBROIDERED ROSE HAIRS

The realistic touch of drawing in the rose hairs, or embroidering them, is typical of the classic Baltimore Album Quilts. Clearly it was the latest style, made possible by the introduction of India ink. One suspects that those who were nervous about inking embellishments, embroidered them onto their classic Album Quilt Blocks. Sometimes, on a bold graphic pattern such as the Sweetheart Rose Lyre, the stitchery is more visible than fine inked lines, and thus adds a great deal to the design's decorativeness. We'll learn more about inking in the next lesson. Here we will focus on the stitching. This is done by eye, not marked.

In the classic Baltimore Album Quilts, a tremendous amount of decorative stitching, particularly buttonholing, was done in crewel wool. Embroidering our Albums in wool hasn't quite made its full swing back into our style repertoire though, so I prefer cotton sewing thread or the green silk sewing thread used on this block.

The stitch to construct embroidered rose hairs couldn't be simpler. Here is how it is done:

1. With a knotted thread, bring the needle up from behind the background fabric 1/4" to 1/3" above the outermost point of a hair (Figure 6-4A).

2. Take a 1/8" stitch at the rose hair's right, making sure the needle comes up over the tail of your thread (Figure 6-4B).

3. Put the needle back in at the calyx's edge (Figure 6-4C). Complete this stitch as you begin the next hair with Step 1 again.

Another pattern for using folded fabric roses: "Brenda's Rosebud Wreath," Pattern #12, with folded rectangle roses. This pattern is much simpler than what you've just done and is a charming original in nineteenth-century style by Brenda Papadakis.

NOTES

[1]Sienkiewicz, Elly, "My Baltimore Album Quilt Discoveries," *Quilter's Newsletter Magazine*, #202, pp. 26-27.

LESSON 7:

Interrupted Cutwork, Plus Stuffed Silk Roses (Stuffed Appliqué), Layered Roses, Cutwork Roses, Simplifying Units in Layered Appliqué, Template-free Flowers, Use of Tie-dyed fabric, and Drawing on Your Block in Ink

PATTERN:

"Lyre Wreath," Pattern #23 (Photo 17)

Lyre Wreath blocks were extremely popular in the Baltimore Album Quilts. One of the most frequent versions frames Baltimore's monument to George Washington, the classic model for our block, as shown in Photo 5. The basic pattern appears here with a suggested center as a marriage block. The center of the wreath could provide an elegant frame for a verse or dedication as well.

"Interrupted cutwork" is such a pedestrian name for the technique that gave us the elegant blocks appearing on both the front and back book covers. It is, however, appropriately descriptive. In both blocks, the green wreath stems and all the same color leaves were appliquéd from *one* square of green cloth.

The wreaths, the leaves, almost all are "interrupted" by flowers layered on top of them. One can't even see the whole shape—just interrupted parts show. In these places, you will sew 1/4" more leaf or stem to extend under the flower. Instructions for marking your green leaf/lyre stem unit are included in "Part Four: The Patterns."

APPLIQUÉ METHOD—
INTERRUPTED CUTWORK

You could carefully approach this block by working on a light table and basting individual elements in place, or by marking your background block for adding appliqué motifs later. But if you are smitten with cutwork, you can hear it calling to you, saying, "Go to your lightbox. Trace what you can see of the wreath and of most of the leaves onto a 13 1/2" piece of green. You know it will take only minutes. And then you and I are free to enjoy each other's company. I will hold everything perfectly in place, and you can appliqué away to your heart's content."

"But what do I do when my appliqué dead-ends under a flower?" you ask, puzzled.

"Why, you just add on 1/4" beyond a leaf or stem for layering under the flower. Look, I even

PHOTO 17. "Lyre Wreath," Pattern #23. Appliqué, fabric selection, pattern adaptation by Joy Nichols; pattern drafting, calligraphy, and Joy Nichol's signature by Elly Sienkiewicz; 1988. (Photo: G. Staley)

drafted a pattern (#23, detail) especially for you to trace onto the green square, to show you what I mean. Come on, soon you're going to have to think a lot, be quick on your toes, make a lot of choices with all those fussy little flower units. The time is fast approaching when we can't be together. 'What is life if full of care, we have no time to stand and stare?'[1] Sit here. Relax with me."

When Cutwork said this to me, I was lost. A verse from an old sundial flashed through my mind—"Time flies. Sun rises. Shadows fall. Let time go by. Love is forever, over all." That was it. There are all sorts of pretty ways to appliqué in this world, but cutwork has my heart.

Stuffed silk roses:
What a delightful surprise to find that these beautiful stuffed silk roses aren't fussy at all! They are easy. In fact, now that you are experienced with needleturn, you can just straight-pin a freezer paper rose pattern to your silk, cut 3/16" beyond it (Figure 7-1A), and needleturn under 1/8" by eye (Figure 7-1B).

Why turn under just 1/8" on a 3/16" seam? Because you'll be pushing back a little to your pattern's turn line, trying to appliqué a slightly bigger shape to a marginally smaller space. This gives a puff of extra room for stuffing.

Stuffing appliqué is literally child's play. Leave a 3/4" opening (at the smoothest spot) as you appliqué around the motif (Figure 7-1C). Then gently stuff in a small, pleasing amount of

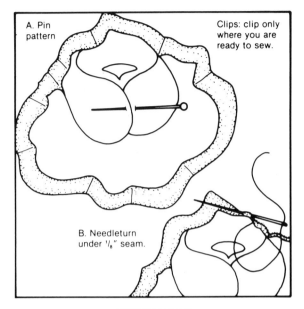

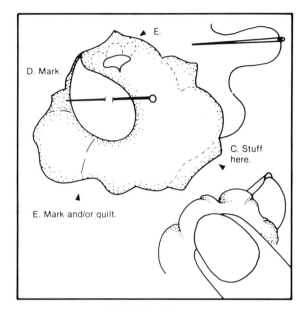

FIGURES 7-1A & 7-1B   FIGURES 7-1C, 7-1D, & 7-1E

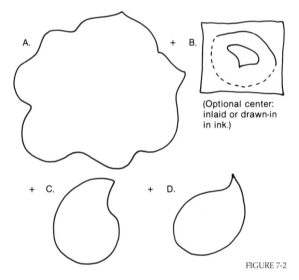

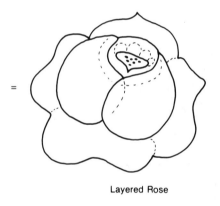

FIGURE 7-2

polyester fiber, and complete your appliqué. Make your life easy by picking the smoothest spot to leave open, so that it is easy to appliqué back up again.

The genius of these particular silk roses is that they are quilted to petalled effect, rather than creating petals by the longer process of layered appliqué. Some are marked for quilting by lines drawn in ink, some have no markings, just the quilted line. Use the same pattern transfer process for both.

1. Cut a freezer paper rose pattern for each of the two main petals which wrap the rose's center (Figure 7-1D).

2. To ink, pin one petal pattern in place on the rose, then brush the lines in delicately with the pen. Practice on the silk beforehand. Repeat for the second petal.

3. The brief lines of the lower petals, and the scalloped inner petals were done by eye (Figure 7-1E). Practice by tracing on paper or on an unsewn silk rose. I always do my inking last. My friend Kate Fowle, who does exquisite work, is cautious and inks first.

4. For the undrawn quilting lines, I pin a freezer paper petal in place and quilt

—Freezer paper pattern ironed on.
—Trim seam to ⅛". Clip.

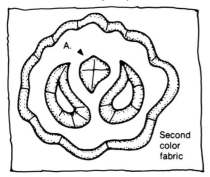

B. Pin-baste to 3" square of second color

FIGURES 7-3A & 7-3B

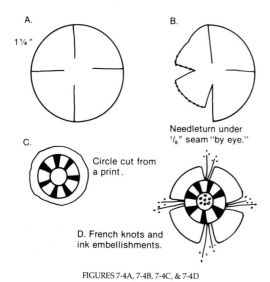

FIGURES 7-4A, 7-4B, 7-4C, & 7-4D

around it. This sounds a bit uncertain, but you will find it works and gives you a practiced eye.

Layered roses:
Some layered appliqué motifs can be completed in your hands before being sewn down to the larger piece. Layered roses can be made in one color or several shades. Appliqué the petals from base to top petal in sequence (Figure 7-2). Then, needleturn this finished unit to the background.

Cutwork roses:
These are simply roses prepared for needleturn appliqué with the freezer paper pattern ironed on top (Lesson 5). Or, if you prefer, they can have the pattern simply traced onto them.

1. Trim back to a 1/8" to 1/16" seam allowance. On some cutwork roses, this will

mean simply a slit or a cross for interior cuts (Figure 7-3A). Clip seams as needed.

2. Pin-baste the rose to a 3" square of the underneath color fabric. Holding this unit comfortably in your hand, do the inlaid (reverse) appliqué. Then trim the second color back before appliquéing your rose to the background fabric (Figure 7-3B).

TEMPLATE-FREE FLOWERS

These flowers are a layered appliqué motif which has to be created on the background fabric. No problem—they are a sheer delight:

1. All they are is a circle (1 1/4" in diameter) slashed to 1/8" of the center in three or sometimes four places (Figure 7-4A). Eventually you can just cut out rough circles by eye, making them truly template-free.

2. Needleturn under all the raw edges by eye, using 1/8" seam (Figure 7-4B).

3. Cut a decorative circle from a print. Appliqué it down as the flower's center (Figure 7-4C).

4. Draw on the ink embellishments and top off with yellow sewing thread French knots (Figure 7-4D). I call these simple flowers "forget-me-nots" and make lots of them because they are so easy.

USING TIE-DYED FABRIC

When we analyze the visual appeal of such simple flowers as these forget-me-nots, it is all in the fabric used. Tie-dyed fabric imitates the shaded rainbow fabrics which are one of the identifying marks of a classic Baltimore Album Quilt. They add the same enhancing depth and hand-painted look to our "Beyond" quilts as they do in the classic Baltimore Album Quilts. Adding a small unit of one print to make a flower more realistic, like the forget-me-not's center, is a bloom right out of "Mary Evans'" garden.

DRAWING ON YOUR BLOCK IN INK

See "Part One: Getting Started" for information on permanent pens; Lesson 3 also has some useful hints about writing on quilts. Your "Rose Lyre" pattern includes all the inked details. The inked hairs on the rose calyx and stems, the veins on the leaves, the inking on the rose blossoms, all are typical in blocks attributed in *Baltimore Album Quilts* to Mary Evans (Photo 18).

How the Statue of Liberty was inked: This may be helpful if you want an image from a photo or a line drawing in the center of your Lyre Wreath.

The Statue of Liberty was traced over a lightbox directly onto the background fabric. The base was traced onto realistically shaded tie-dyed cotton.[2] I traced the statue from a photocopy (of a photograph) which had in turn been photocopied numerous times. This gave the final photocopy a grainy texture, more like a simplified engraving. To trace it onto fabric, I used very few lines, mainly dots. To color it, I brushed on a wash of green and bronze acrylic paint, then heat-set the whole with an iron.

Another pattern to make using interrupted cutwork: "Silhouette Wreath," Pattern #16. This is a more complex green wreath than the Lyre. See the classic original in Photo 6.

PHOTO 18. White silk rose with inked inner petals and stamens. From the center medallion square of a Baltimore Album Quilt inscribed "To / Miss Elizabeth Sliver / This is Affections tribute Offering- / Presented By Father & Mother / To / Miss Elizabeth Sliver / Baltimore- 1849."*Baltimore Album Quilts* attributes this quilt to the person "traditionally identified as Mary Evans." Note the undulating print which, in the three uppermost right-hand leaves, has been cut from a stripe and splits the center of the leaf like a vein. Also, typical of nineteenth-century appliqué in general, no fabric has been cut out from behind the rose. (Photo: The Baltimore Museum of Art: Gift of the Friends of the American Wing. BMA 1976.93)

NOTES

[1] William Henry Davies.

[2] This fabric was tie-dyed by Patricia Gill.

LESSON 8:

Mixed Appliqué Techniques, Ruching, and the Textured-edge Running Stitch, Plus Needleturning Without a Marked Seam Turn Line, Nineteenth-century Style

PATTERN:
"Ruched Rose Lyre," Pattern #24 (Photo 19)

Ruched Rose Lyre is a "wonderful to look at, delightful to make" block. The design is simple, so you must pick sophisticated prints and subtle colors to make it most effective. Because the shapes are large and graphic, this block sets off fancier blocks well.

Ruched Rose Lyre teaches us many things: how to use onlaid cutwork and individual motif appliqué on the same wreath stem, how to speed stitch, how to add a textured edge with top stitch appliqué, and how to ruche a flower. Moreover, it is fast, easy, and fun to make.

BLOCK PREPARATION/
PATTERN TRANSFER

See "Part One: Getting Started" for details of transfering patterns that are given as a whole block in the pattern section ("Part Four: The Patterns").

1. Work on a lightbox. Mark the wreath stem (and the nine leaves attached to it) on a square of green fabric for unit cutwork appliqué.

2. Pin-baste this marked green cloth to the background fabric.

3. From three or four other prints or variegated plain fabrics (such as shaded or tie-dyed material), cut more of the separate leaf units than the nine needed so you'll have some choice. To make these, follow the instructions in Step 4.

4. Mark *half* of these leaves with the turn line and trim to 1/8" seam beyond it. For the other leaves, make a paper leaf template which *includes* the 1/8" seam. Pin this template to the fabric and cut around it. These leaves will be needleturned by eye, nineteenth-century style.

PHOTO 19. "Ruched Rose Lyre," Pattern #24. Appliqué, pattern drafting, fabric selection, calligraphy, and signature by Elly Sienkiewicz, 1988. (Photo: D. Sienkiewicz)

5. Cut a 45" x 1 1/4" strip of a subtly shaded monochromatic print for your ruched, "full-blown rose." Or use a splendid solid-color fabric with highlights: a silk or satin, an iridescent taffeta, or the wonderful rayon found for this block.

   This fabric does not need to be cut on the bias if it is a soft, fine cotton, or silk, silk satin, or a synthetic. My first ruched flowers were made of rayon seam tape, surely the easy way out. You can see them in the Vase of Fancy Flowers, block D-2 in quilt #6.

   Close up, the fabric is clearly a synthetic, as is my rose in this block. To me, these are proud reflections of twentieth-century technology in a quilt with classic traditions. Some, however, may prefer to stick to natural fibers. Real silk is pure luxury and was used in precious small quantities in the classic Baltimore Album Quilts. The white silk roses found in Baltimore-style quilts are famous in themselves.

PROCEDURE

1. Refer to Lesson 5 on unit cutwork. Use this method to complete the entire outside and inside of the stem and all those leaves which the pattern shows as attached to the

stem. Begin at the top outside seam of the left-hand wreath-stem if you are right-handed. Begin at the top inside seam if you are left-handed.

2. When all the cutwork is appliquéd, mark your background fabric. Work on a lightbox. Mark, with a dot, the top and bottom point of each leaf to be added on separately. While you are at it, mark the dotted lines which guide sewing the center of the ruched strip. Include the "X" which marks where you start attaching the ruching.

3. Arrange the remaining leaf units on the block in a pleasing color arrangement. Pin through the points of the leaf into the dots of the background fabric. The pattern is true. Some of the leaves abut the stem, some overlap it. This was done intentionally for decorative effect.

4. Baste before you begin to appliqué. Small units have an uncanny tendency to shift out of place. Basting makes you appreciate just how much the uncut cloth of cutwork appliqué has been holding the units in place, and how much work it saved you on the attached wreaths and leaves from Lessons 5, 6, and 7.

APPLIQUÉ'S SPEED STITCH

Three stitches are used on this block:

1. The slow, versatile tack stitch for cutwork needleturn appliqué, and for appliquéing the ruching down.

2. The quicker blind stitch, if you like, on the curves of the leaves.

3. A textured-edge running stitch for speedy, decorative top-stitch appliqué. This latter is the very fastest appliqué stitch and adds a textured edge to those leaves which are appliquéd as separate motifs. This texture makes a nice sculptural balance to the very three-dimensional ruching.

Jean Ray Laury, a prodigious appliqué designer and delightful teacher, introduced so many of

us to running stitch appliqué. Jeanne Benson, who combines a refined design sense with exceptionally innovative appliqué, introduced me to the idea of the "textured edge" created by tiny quilted appliqué stitches defining a motif's outline in appealing rhythm. The stitch is the same by any name: running, quilting, speed, or textured edge. It was so quick and simple that I had saved it for patching children's clothes. Jean and Jeanne elevated it to art needlework. To my knowlege, it does not appear in the classic Appliqué Album Quilts and is thus, "Beyond Baltimore."

Needleturning more seam under before continuing running stitch appliqué.

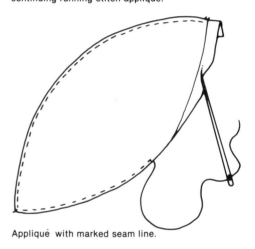

Appliqué with marked seam line.

FIGURE 8-1

Needleturn with no marked seam line: nineteenth-century style.

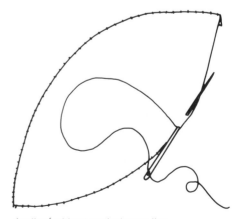

Appliqué without marked seam line.

FIGURE 8-2

APPLIQUÉING WITH THE TEXTURED-EDGE RUNNING STITCH

Use this for the leaves whose turn line you have marked.

1. Hold the fabric so that the folded edge is away from you. Needleturn under the 1/8" seam. Start at the top point, as shown in Figure 8-1. Lock the point with two tiny tack stitches. Then sew even, little running stitches right next to the fold, all the way to the bottom of the leaf.

2. At the bottom point, take two tack stitches through the fold. Swing the seam allowance under and into the point, against these strong anchor stitches. Then resume your running stitches. Finish the top point with a couple of tight tack stitches.

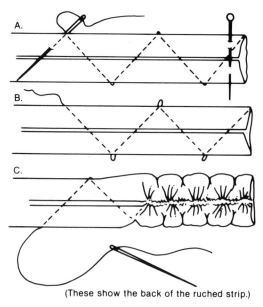

(These show the back of the ruched strip.)

FIGURES 8-3A, 8-3B, & 8-3C

APPLIQUÉING BY NEEDLETURN APPLIQUÉ

Try needleturning under by eye these leaves with the unmarked 1/8" seam. It isn't hard (Figure 8-2). In addition, the process provides some insight into how the classic Baltimore Album Quilts were made.

A seam-included template speeds up the pattern transfer process. There is no marking to do. Appliqué motifs prepared this way could be stack-cut. This would be the first step for production appliqué.

Unmarked fabric shapes (*including* tiny seam allowances), basted onto the background block for needleturning, seem to be the way separate unit appliqué was done in the classic Baltimore Album Quilt period. The basted "Mary Evans" block pictured in "Part One: Getting Started" (Photo 4) shows no marked turn line although the block itself has "pencil marks."[1]

I have studied other unfinished blocks[2] of this vintage and scrutinized classic Baltimore Album Quilts for any signs of marked turn or cutting lines, and have found none. More thoughts on the possibly important implications of this are in Lesson 12.

HOW TO RUCHE YOUR "FULL-BLOWN ROSE"

Of all the forgotten techniques presented by the classic Album Quilts, perhaps the most perplexing was "ruching." Even expert researchers among us were stumped. Massive dictionaries and erudite encyclopedias didn't really help the frustrated needlewoman. "Decorative, gathered fabric" simply wasn't an adequately technical description of how the realistic zinnia, chrysanthemum, or full-blown rose-like flowers were made.

We were all too curious for this situation to last long. Betty Boyink reported that a friend had gently pulled back ruching on an antique quilt[3] and had seen what appeared to be a meandering line of stitches. Clara Slembarski later shared her turn-of-the-century needlework book with me. It illustrated this basic principle of ruching: The running stitch is sewn in a regular, repeated right-angle zigzag pattern along the length of a 1 1/4"-wide (raw edges in) fabric strip. These stitches are then pulled to gather, or "ruched." This ruched strip is sewn in a concentric circle to form a flower. Here's the process in more detail:

1. Fold 1/4" under along both sides at the right-hand end of your 45" x 1 1/4" fabric strip. Or simply fold the raw edges in until they just touch in the center. Pin to hold.

2. Stitch eight to ten stitches per inch in the zigzag right-angle pattern shown in Figure 8-3A. This is a familiar enough pattern that you can follow it by eye. Fold in the seams as you sew along.

3. When you sew to the fold, always loop your thread over the fold before you begin to stitch in the other direction (Figure 8-3B).

This gives a good strong differentiation to the rhythm of puckered petals which will be formed when you pull your thread. (Hint: Use a fine, but longer needle, and a strong thread.)

4. Sew about 8", then gently pull your thread to gather the fabric into puckers. Your line of stitches will be pulled straight, resulting in petal-puffs on either side (Figure 8-3C).

5. Before continuing to ruche, tack down what you have already gathered. You will first baste your ruching down (Steps A through C below), then appliqué it down (Step D):
   a. The front of the ruched strip faces you. Its seams are to the back (Figure 8-4).
   b. Tuck the first 1/4" raw-edged end under. Tack it to the "X" mark on your background fabric. Do this tacking with a second needle (not the running stitch one) threaded in the rose's color (Figure 8-4).
   c. Continue to baste the ruched strip down its length to the background fabric. Use the concentric circles marked on your background fabric as a rough guide. When the strip moves down into a second ring, the previous ring's outer petals should overlap the next ring's inner petals.
   d. Now pull your basting needle back to the center and appliqué your ruching down with it. Appliqué with one tack stitch in the center of each petal as it overlaps the next row down. This is your chance to make the spacing of the petals pleasing (Figure 8-5). Park your needle where the overlapping stops. At this point, resume Steps 2 through 4 until the whole 45" is ruched.

6. On the outer rim of the rose, tuck the raw-edge end of your ruching strip under the nearest petal and secure it as you finish appliquéing your rose down. Ruching should look neat, regular, and wonderfully flowerlike. Congratulations on a beautiful rose.

ALTERNATE RUCHING INSTRUCTIONS

I've done all my ruching by the above process, but if you prefer to leave less to the eye, try these more exacting instructions:

FIGURE 8-4

Appliqué ruching down with a tack stitch in each petal.

FIGURE 8-5

Iron 1/4" seam in on either side of your long fabric strip. A bias seam maker is a handy gadget which aids this process greatly. Next iron in the right-angle folds. To do this, fold the fabric back on itself in repeated right angles to place the folds (Figure 8-6).

Does this look familiar? This was how we made pop-out figures in kindergarten: jack-in-the-boxes, and those zany pumpkin or valentine people with pop-out arms and legs. Little did we know then what a useful technique we were learning. Begin ruching with Step 3, above.

Another ruched rose pattern to make: "Token of Gratitude," Pattern #17. This features ruched roses

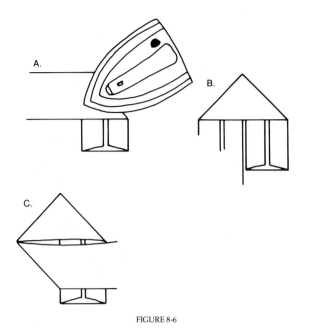

A.

B.

C.

FIGURE 8-6

and folded half-circle roses. This pattern is like a Master's exam, but Dot Reise made our glorious sample block with very little previous appliqué experience!

NOTES

[1] *Baltimore Album Quilts*, p. 53.

[2] Sienkiewicz, Elly, "My Baltimore Album Quilt Discoveries," *Quilter's Newsletter Magazine*, #202, pp. 26-27.

[3] Boyink, Betty, *Flower Gardens and Hexagons for Quilters.* This book contains many more three-dimensional flower ideas.

LESSON 9:

Superfine Stems, Stuffed Berries, and Perfect Grapes, Plus Split Leaves

PATTERN:
"Crown of Laurel/Broken Wreath of Cherries," Pattern #18 (Photo 20)

Appropriately symbolic, highly decorative, and pleasing to make, berries are the prevalent fruit in the classic Baltimore Album Quilts. Currants, laurel berries, cherries, grapes, and strawberries all appear in cheerful abundance.

BLOCK PREPARATION/ PATTERN TRANSFER

See "Part One: Getting Started" for details of pattern transfer methods. Mark your 16" background square very lightly with one dot where the stem touches the cherry, and with one dot where it touches the wreath-stem. Mark one dot at every leaf-tip, top and bottom. Very lightly draw, as solid lines, the dotted lines at the outside of the wreath and around the berries.

PROCEDURE

Make the cherry stems first, then the wreath or "crown-stem," next the leaves, and finally the cherries.

Making superfine stems:
"Superfine stems" are easy, quick, and have the beautiful look of trapuntoed appliqué. They can be found on nineteenth-century quilts and have a tell-tale stuffed look. This look comes from the four layers which are stuffed into stems made this way.

I have not yet noticed these stems in a classic Baltimore Album Quilt. In addition, the lesson of the unfinished Sands House Appliqué Album Quilt blocks is that simple needleturning on either side of a 1/2" strip may have been the stem method which prevailed during that period. Nonetheless, superfine stems are too useful to ignore.

Begin by making a sample stem first:

1. Make a pattern by cutting a 3" x 3/4" masking tape strip. Press it onto the bias of your stem fabric (Figure 9-1).

PHOTO 20. "Crown of Laurel/Broken Wreath of Cherries," Pattern #18. Appliqué, fabric placement, and chain-stitched signature by Ann Peters; pattern drafting and fabric selection by Elly Sienkiewicz; 1988. (Photo: D. Sienkiewicz)

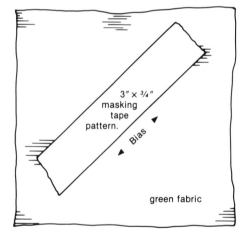

FIGURE 9-1

2. Cut the 3" x 3/4" strip, marked by the masking tape, out of your green fabric.

3. Fold this piece of green bias in half lengthwise, wrong sides together. Baste it (down its center length) to a piece of background fabric. The folded edge is to your left, the raw edges are to your right (Figure 9-2).

4. With tiny running stitches, sew the length of the strip, along the right of your basting stitches (Figure 9-2). These stitches become the left-hand seam of your stem and can also be machine stitched.

5. Press the folded edge to the right, back over the raw edge. Trim the raw edge a bit if necessary. Appliqué the fold down (Figure 9-3).

Superfine stem principles are simple:

1. To make even the finest stem, never use a piece of bias smaller than 3/4" wide. You are a "giant" for the task at hand. Do your sewing on a normal scale, then trim the seam.

2. The width of your stem is equal to the distance between your folded edge and the parallel line of running stitches.

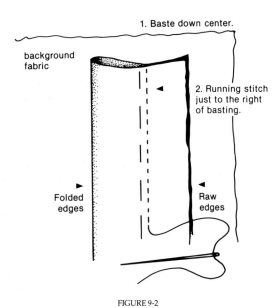

1. Baste down center.

background fabric

2. Running stitch just to the right of basting.

Folded edges

Raw edges

FIGURE 9-2

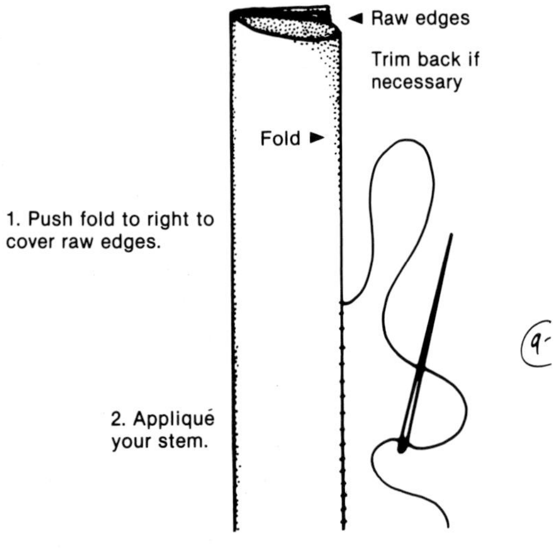

◄ Raw edges

Trim back if necessary

Fold ►

1. Push fold to right to cover raw edges.

2. Appliqué your stem.

FIGURE 9-3

3. Your raw edges always face the outside (the larger side) of your curve. Thus, when you push your bias fold *back* over the seam allowance, it will stretch to cover the larger curve.

Sewing the stems onto the block:

1. Pin the folded bias strip onto your block (Figure 9-4).

2. The bias' fold faces the left (or down) on stems inside the wreath. It faces the right (or down) on stems on the outside of the wreath.

3. The strip follows the stem's shape from 1/4" (the layering seam allowance) above the dot at the cherry, to 1/4" beyond the dot where the stem touches the wreath (Figure 9-4). The excess strip is trimmed off after sewing.

4. This stem is 1/8" wide. Thus the distance from the fold to the dots must be 1/8." Your seam runs from dot to dot (Figure 9-4, also).

5. Sew the seam. Trim the raw edge back very close to your running stitches. Press the folded edge over the raw edges and appliqué it down (Figure 9-3).

   Hint: Bias consumes fabric. Choose one yard of the dominant green in your quilt. Iron it in half diagonally to mark the line for cutting this first bias strip with the masking tape pattern. Then save the two

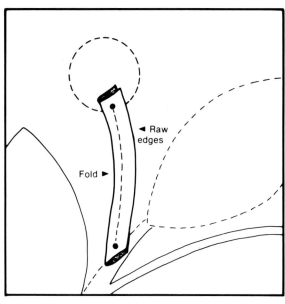

◄ Raw edges

Fold ►

FIGURE 9-4

large triangles of fabric for cutting all future bias strips.

Many, many of our Baltimore sisters of yore sidestepped this whole issue of uneconomical fabric use by cutting stems on the straight. You can economize by cutting leaves from one corner of this yard, but preserve the nice long bias edge for all the wreaths and nosegays your heart may desire.

Making the crown-stems:
After all the cherry stems are sewn, make the crossed crown-stems. These will cover the bottom of every cherry stem. They are made on the same principle as the cherry stems:

1. Using 3/4" masking tape as your guide, cut a 3/4" x 30" strip of green bias.

2. Fold the strip in half lengthwise, right-side out, as above. Pin to the top of the left crown-stem 1/4" under where the leaf will go. Raw edges are just touching the dotted line; the fold is facing to the right.

3. The very fastest, easiest way to sew a long, curved stem is on the sewing machine. With your left hand you need only guide the raw edges to touch the drawn line, while your machine's presser foot helps guide your stitches to run 3/16" parallel to the fold.
    If you sew with tight stitches in the same color thread, no one in a hundred years will know this seam was sewn on the machine. And if, in a hundred years, they figure it out, you will have given them the thrill of discovery! Nonetheless, you may prefer to sew running stitches by hand as described above.

4. At the bottom of this crown-stem, cut the excess strip off to use on the opposite, overlapping stem. Finish by appliquéing stem ends and the folded stem edges down, as before. Once this is done, the leaves which abut or overlap the stem should be tackled.

The leaves:
Make the leaves for this block as you did those in Lesson 8. You may want to include split leaves, a variation found in some ornate Victorian-style blocks (see Photos 4 and 6). These leaves are split in half lengthwise. A different fabric is used on each half. Sometimes a solid color was used on one side, a print on the other. Rarely, but to striking ef-

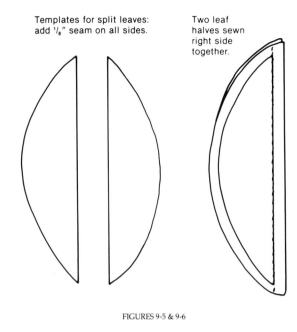

Templates for split leaves: add ¹/₈" seam on all sides.

Two leaf halves sewn right side together.

FIGURES 9-5 & 9-6

fect, bottle-green silk velvet was used on one side, and a cotton print on the other side. In many cases, the "split" look came from the print itself: meandering blue-green on one side, buff on the other, as though the leaves were cut from two adjacent stripes.

Good leaves for doing in two colors are the ones which touch (but don't go over or under) the wreath stem. Use the template (Figure 9-5) to cut leaf halves. Add 1/8" seam all around and sew a pair together (Figure 9-6). Needleturn appliqué the seamed leaf to the background fabric.

Mix your print and plain fabrics, your soft mediums and lights and darks in an appealing decorative effect, as though you were painting. Often this variety, as in our model, is sufficient, without adding split leaves. With the leaves accomplished, you are ready to cultivate your berries. Ann Peters made the beautiful block pictured in Photo 20 and used the following method for the slightly stuffed berries.

Joy Nichols' method for stuffed berries:
Bushels of berries can be seen stuffed on the classic Baltimore Album Quilts. Joy Nichols, whose needle-talent is happily linked with exquisite taste in fabric and embellishment, shares this secret of how she stuffs a perfect berry.

1. Use a quarter coin as a template. Drawing around its perimeter gives you the sewing line. Cut the circle out 1/8" beyond this line. If you choose silk, which is slippery, mark, stitch, and stuff the berry on a larger scrap first, before trimming off to the seam

allowance. Hint: If you use silk, get good quality silk such as China Silk. Silk that is made as a lining material is just too thin and fragile for an heirloom quilt.

2. Using cherry-colored thread, take small running stitches all around your drawn

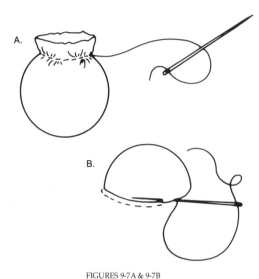

FIGURES 9-7A & 9-7B

PHOTO 21. "Grapevine Wreath," appliqué, fabric selection, and stem-stitch embroidered signature by Zollalee Gaylor, 1985; quilting by Carol White, 1987; pattern drafting by Elly Sienkiewicz, 1983. This 12 1/2" block appliqué pattern appears in *Spoken Without a Word*. The original block is in a Baltimore Album Quilt dated 1843-45 (from a private collection), and is shown as quilt #1 in *Baltimore Album Quilts*. Beautifully repetitive like a wrought-iron design, this is an early classic Album Quilt grapevine wreath. At the height of the classic period, asymmetry and more fluidity seem to characterize these wreaths. This block is E-2 in quilt #6 in the Color Section. (Photo: S. Sienkiewicz)

circle. The seam allowance is not turned under.

3. When you're back to where you started, tug the thread to gather. Push a thimbleful of polyester fiber into the pocket you've just made. Add a little, more or less as needed, to make a plump, tight cherry (Figure 9-7A).

4. Pull your thread tight and stay stitch. Now, with the same threaded needle, appliqué your succulent cherry to the marked circle line, using the blind stitch. Following this drawn pattern should force the stuffed circle into a "perfect cherry" (Figure 9-7B).

Perfect small circles or grapes:
In those classic Album Blocks which I have been able to look at closely, the grapes, cherries, and circle berries of any sort seem to have been needleturned under, most with a tack stitch.

In the 1846-47 "Currant Wreath with Blue Birds" (block D-2 in quilt #4), red currants are sewn down with off-white thread. The stitches are fine, approximately 15-17 per inch, but not hidden. There is no evidence of a drawn turn line, but the berries are beautifully turned circles, virtually perfect grapes. One has insight into this needlewoman of yore as one reads these words from our contemporary, Zollalee Gaylor:

"My technique is very simple. I use nothing more than needle and thread working the material the way I want it to go. I always work clockwise around the patch using the needle to stroke, push, poke and turn the fabric. I keep the needle coming towards me so I can see exactly where it is. I use a size 12 needle which keeps the stitches small and helps to limit the threads picked up as the needle comes up through the edge of the patch.

"I feel my circles and vines turn out quite good. To see the grapes on my block, it would be hard to see how the lopsided templates I made could turn out a patch so round. A lot of it I attribute to a good eye. Otherwise I have no secret, except practice. The seam allowance acts as padding."[1]

So many people, looking at Zollalee's Grapevine Wreath from quilt #6 (Photo 21), have been full of admiration and questions. "How did she make those grapes so perfect?" and "Are they stuffed?" Zollalee's candid answer is straightforward and helpful. And so simple.

Looked at closely, on top of a lightbox, the aforementioned heart-shaped Currant Wreath block showed no evidence that a paper template of any sort had been used inside the berries (unless pulled out at the end). There was no cutting out of background fabric from behind any of the appliqués in this classic Baltimore Album Quilt, nor has there been in any nineteenth-century quilts that I have been able to discern.

All evidence that I have been able to observe in the classic Baltimore Album Quilts, points to one customary method of appliquéing units: The fabric was cut out in the desired shape, then the edge was needleturned under, 1/8" to 1/16" by eye alone, with no seam line marked. Creating a perfectly turned circle by eye takes practice. The good Ladies of Baltimore certainly had that, and so will you.

ONCE OVER LIGHTLY ON OTHER PERFECT CIRCLE METHODS

Needleturning a circle takes the least preparation of any circle-making method. But many people are devoted to other methods which they feel are both faster and easier. Most of the additional ways to make a "perfect grape" involve using one of the ten seam-basted-under appliqué techniques covered in Lesson 10. Here are two variations not discussed there.

Variation One:
Cut a plastic grape template. Baste your seam over the back of it, sewing back and forth. Leave the template in while you appliqué the grape. When finished, slit the back of the background fabric and pinch the appliqué; the template, being flexible plastic, will pop out. (This trick was shown to me by Jeana Kimball.)

Variation Two:
Cut a file card template. This version has the advantage that the slit needed to pull the pliable paper template out (use a straight pin) is smaller. Still others gather the seam around a file card template with running stitches, like a yo-yo.

All these techniques, each different, and each one so sincerely advocated by such good appliqué artists...it all points to us being creatures of habit and reinforces the maxim "Practice makes perfect." A similarly diverse loyalty is true of stem-making methods as well.

ONCE OVER LIGHTLY ON OTHER SUPER STEM METHODS

Let's start by going back to Zollalee Gaylor's description of her appliqué techniques:

"To make vines I cut bias and fold it right side out. I sew a seam the finished width from the fold side and trim the raw edges close to the seam. If wide enough, the seam is rolled to the back. For the vines in the Strawberry Wreath,[2] I appliquéd the folded edge down first.

"I like to feel that I'm carrying on the tradition begun by those ladies in Baltimore so long ago. If I had a time machine, I would love to visit one of their sewing circles and compare my work with theirs. I hope they would consider my work good enough to be included in one of their Bride's Quilts."

There is no doubt in my mind that the good Ladies of Baltimore would have loved having the work of Zollalee and the so many other skilled needleworkers who are plying their needles across the country in an overwhelmingly beautiful Baltimore Album Quilt revival.

Kate Fowle also has a clever technique. She cuts a 1/2" bias strip, smears one long side with a glue stick, presses an 1/8" seam to it, repeats the process on the other side, then re-glues the back of the whole stem and irons it to her background cloth, using the ironed-dry glue (from the glue stick) for adhesion.

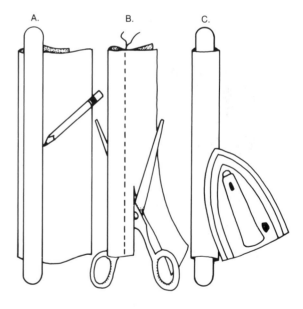

FIGURES 9-8A, 9-8B, & 9-8C

"Bias bar" stems:
Philomena Wiechek made elegant Celtic appliqué possible with her versatile notion, "bias bars." Use these, first as a template to mark the seam of folded-in-half bias strips for machining (Figures 9-8A and 9-8B), and then as "ironing boards" (slipped inside the tube) to iron the strip with the seam hidden behind it (Figure 9-8C).

The interwoven red baskets sometimes found in the most ornate Baltimore quilts must have been done in a similar way. This question puzzled me. They had no Philomena back then. Then it struck me that they had the bias bar's prototype: the corset stay. So I like to call strips made this way, "corset-stay bias." (For a red basket which you can weave, see Lesson 12.)

In the Sands House blocks, that serendipitous find[3] of unfinished blocks from mid-nineteenth-century Maryland, there are many stems, basted only, to show how their maker planned to proceed. These blocks show basted, 1/2"-wide cloth cut on the straight for both sprays of flowers and the circles of wreaths. Near one basted block's ribbon, the seam is turned under (1/8" on either side), ready to sew. There are no marked turn lines. A small, black, geometric print, though, seems to be serving, still, as the guide for turning the seam (Photo 22). That it still awaits the sewing and is yet so treasured should comfort all of us with unfinished projects.

I was charmed to find that bouquet's ribbon actually tied around these stems. No doubt the maker was delighted with her clever treatment and had turned under just enough stem seams at the ribbon's edge to see what the effect would be.

PHOTO 22. One of several circa 1850 basted Album Quilt blocks from the Sands House, the oldest wooden house in Annapolis, Maryland. Notice the bits of shaded blue rainbow fabric pieced to form each petal of the clematis-like flower and the pansies. Perhaps this tiny bit of characteristically Baltimore Album Quilt fabric was a treasure from Baltimore, 25 miles or so away. Geometric (black print on green) calicoes in these unfinished blocks closely resemble some in quilt #4, shown in the Color Section. (Photo: S. Sienkiewicz, courtesy M. Dowsett)

One last stem method, one last glorious challenge:
In the falcon block from her appliqué Album, "Nancy's Garden,"[4] Nancy Pearson appears to have done branches, leaves, stems, in inlaid appliqué. It looks wonderful in Nancy's block. You have already done some well-wrought stems and leaves in onlaid cutwork. So we are back full circle to inlaid or onlaid cutwork for stems. So many choices. What a delightful thought for a winter day: Fill a quilt with flowers and try them all!

Another superfine stem and berry pattern to make: "Wreath of Cherries," Pattern #11. This pattern is lavishly graphic. Our model was painstakingly made by Roberta Floyd.

NOTES

[1] Zollalee made two masterpiece berry blocks, blocks E-2 and E-3 in quilt #6. Her helpful words are taken from the questionnaire she filled out "About the Needleartists" for this book.

[2] Block E-3 in quilt #6. The 12 1/2" pattern for this circa 1843-45 block is given in *Spoken Without a Word,* p. 50.

[3] Sienkiewicz, Elly, "My Baltimore Album Quilt Discoveries," *Quilter's Newsletter Magazine,* #202, pp. 26-27.

[4] *Forget Me Not,* p. 119.

LESSON 10:

The Many Modes of Seams Pre-basted-under Appliqué, Including Turn and Baste, Machine-edged Turn Line, English Paper Method, English Paper Method with Freezer Paper, Spray Appliqué, Freezer Paper Inside, Freezer Paper Inside with Glue Stick, [Plastic] Template Appliqué™, Yo-yo Hearts, and Basted Reverse Appliqué

PATTERN:

"Wreath of Hearts I," Pattern #19. This pattern is pure "Baltimore," from a circa 1850 quilt. Our model block (Version II—see Photo 23), however, is a "Beyond Baltimore" block with the addition of hearts, hands, a buttonholed butterfly, and calligraphy. The directions here are for "Wreath of Hearts I."

BLOCK PREPARATION/ PATTERN TRANSFER

Review "Part One: Getting Started" for details of pattern transfer methods for patterns shown at one-half block and for notes on freezer paper. Then, working on a lightbox, mark with a clear dot the convex "V" of each heart, and, where you can see them at the pattern's center, their points.

Have at hand a nice selection of reds and greens. Then work your way through the list of ten methods for seams-pre-basted-under appliqué. Some methods you may just want to read, some you will want to try. The ones that interest you the most, practice. If you feel like it, time yourself on several different methods and see how they compare.

Begin at the heart marked with an "X" on your pattern. Take care following your placement dots, and use the tack or blind stitch. Save the heart just below it until last for basted reverse (inlaid) appliqué (method 10).

Except where basting the prepared appliqué to the background fabric is integral to the method being taught, our directions for each method stop after the appliqué shape is prepared.

SEAMS PRE-BASTED- UNDER APPLIQUÉ

The principle of seams pre-basted-under appliqué is always the same: By separating the tasks of preparing the turned-under seam from the task of appliquéing, you can do both faster and better.

PHOTO 23. "Wreath of Hearts II," Pattern #19. Appliqué, pattern drafting, fabric selection, tracing of George Bickham's eighteenth-century calligraphy, and signature by Elly Sienkiewicz, 1988. (Photo: G. Staley)

Is this in fact the case? In our nation's capital and in its nearby suburbs, there is no doubt that this principle is true: I affectionately refer to this area as "Freezer Paper Heaven." We are lucky to have among our local quiltmakers, Anne Oliver, who close to a dozen years ago discovered and shared the fact that using freezer paper inside the appliqué can speed the process of basted appliqué considerably. Done well it can give a smooth, well-defined edge to the appliqué of a needleworker of even modest skill. The National Capital Area, seemingly as a whole, converted to the "freezer paper inside" method of appliqué.

My passion has always been the opposite category of appliqué: I love all the turn-as-you-go methods we have described in the lessons thus far. When I added my discovery, "freezer paper on top," to my beloved inlaid and onlaid cutwork and simple needleturn, I felt I had finally entered Freezer Paper Heaven myself!

I decided to test the hypothesis that "freezer paper inside" was faster than needleturn appliqué. I was helped here by members of several guilds to whom I've taught the workshop "You've Stolen My Heart: Twelve Appliqué Techniques." Late in the afternoon, after practicing both methods, whoever wanted to timed herself in each method on a heart similar to one from this lesson. The answer surprised, and really pleased, me, for all of us are devoted to doing appliqué "our way." The time spent on each method was virtually the same for everybody.

The difference was that with the "freezer paper inside" method, more preparation time was taken cutting templates and ironing the seam under; the appliqué itself, by whatever stitch one chose, was faster. With onlaid cutwork appliqué, preparation time was shorter, but appliqué combined with cutting and turning the edge under took longer. Both cutwork needleturn and "freezer paper inside" took about the same *total* length of time.

If time is not a factor, and both methods are easy, when is "freezer paper inside" an advantage? From my point of view, it is in designing the fabric use of a multifabric block such as Wreath of Hearts or in designing a block right on your background cloth. Any basted-under appliqué method allows you to see from the start what your finished block will look like—and that is a real thrill.

BASTED APPLIQUÉ METHODS

1. Turn and baste:

This is the method your mother or grandmother probably taught you. Might it have gained popularity from all those pre-printed appliqué kits of half a century ago? Draw the turn line on the right side of the fabric, trim off to a 3/16" seam allowance, and clip to one to two threads at the "V" (Figure 10-1A). Fold back the seam allowance and baste it under, running small stitches close to the fold. **Note:** In all of the following methods you must cut to one to two threads from the turn line at the "V" before turning the seam under, so this instruction won't be repeated.

To miter a corner in pre-basted appliqué, fold the seam allowance point up at a right angle to the drawn point (Figure 10-1B). Fold the right side seam over this as you baste (Figure 10-1C), and then secure the left side to this at the bottom when you finish off your basting (Figure10-1D).

Try the "neat loop" method of tucking-in a point. First, baste the seam under, sewing from the left side down to the point. The right seam folds over the left at the point. When you come basting back up the right side, make sure your thread loops over the bottom of the point (Figure10-2). Take a few stitches, tug, and your still-looped thread pulls the point in neatly.

2. Machine-edged turn line:

Run tight machine stitching just inside the raw-edge side of your drawn sewing line (Figure 10-3). If you are making several hearts from the same fabric, draw and machine stitch them before cutting them out (with a 3/16" seam allowance). These tight stitches define your edge sharply, and are already easing your fabric into a curve. You'll

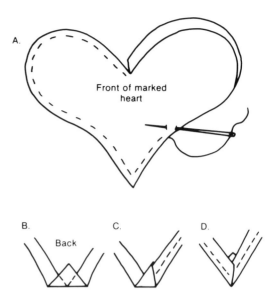

Front of marked heart

Back

FIGURES 10-1A, 10-1B, 10-1C, & 10-1D

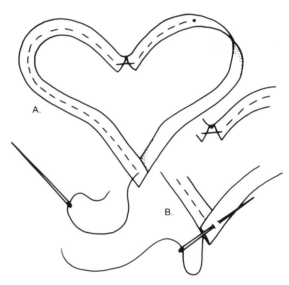

A.

B.

FIGURE 10-2

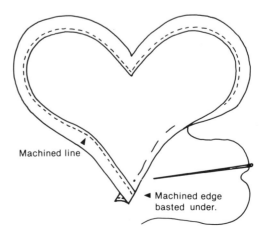

Machined line

Machined edge basted under.

FIGURE 10-3

enjoy the benefit of this when you fold back the seam allowance and baste it to the heart. (Katherine Kuhn notes that she does all of her appliqué this way.)

3. English paper method:
Pin-baste a typing-weight paper template to the wrong side of a 3" square fabric scrap (Figure 10-4). Trim off around this template to 3/16" seam allowance. Holding the appliqué seam side facing you, gently pull the seam over the paper's edge towards you and baste carefully as in Method #1, stitching through the paper template as well. The advantage is that the paper gives a sharp edge to your turn line. Cut the background fabric behind the appliqué to remove the paper.

4. English paper method with freezer paper:
Make a template out of freezer paper, then iron it, shiny side down, on the wrong side of your fabric (Figure 10-5). Trim off to 3/16" seam allowance. Now baste as in Method #1.

5. Spray appliqué:
Pin a heart template cut from a white file card to a 3" scrap of fabric. Pull the excess fabric back against the template. Spray some starch into the lid of the starch can. Then take a cotton swab and dab a little starch onto the turn line. Use a hot, dry iron. Carefully press the fabric over the card's edge in small sweeping strokes, catching the seam smoothly and ironing it down. Remove your template before trimming the seam 3/16" beyond your crisply starched, turned seam (Figure 10-6).

6. Freezer paper inside:
Pin a freezer paper heart, shiny side up, to the wrong side of your fabric. Trim to a 3/16", or smaller, seam. Iron the triangle at the point straight back against the heart (as in Method #1). Long fingernails are a blessing at this juncture. I don't have them, so I use a quilter's pin or an orange stick to hold the heart in place as I iron. Dab glue stick on this triangle. Fingerpress the seams in on either side to be held by the glue (Figure 10-7A). (This hint is courtesy of Kate Fowle.) Iron the heart's side seam edge to the freezer paper with a smooth sweeping motion that catches the seam and pushes it against and over the edge to adhere to the freezer paper. Imagine you are frosting a cake and you want all the swirls to sweep into its center (Figure 10-7B).

The "hump" of the heart and the "V" are the hardest. You are ironing a larger seam allowance of fabric back into a smaller shape. Avoid peaks and puckers. Do a bit of "heat-basting": jab the hot iron's point to fuse the fabric in a few places, then

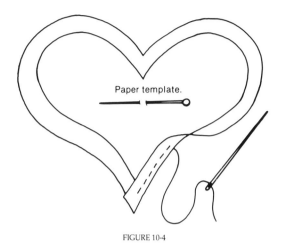

FIGURE 10-4

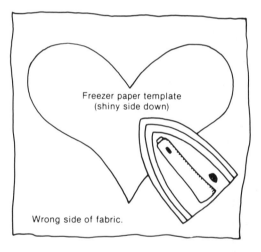

Freezer paper template (shiny side down)

Wrong side of fabric.

FIGURE 10-5

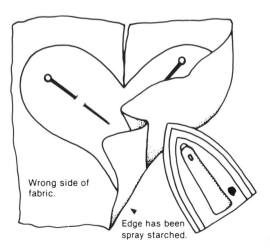

Wrong side of fabric.

Edge has been spray starched.

FIGURE 10-6

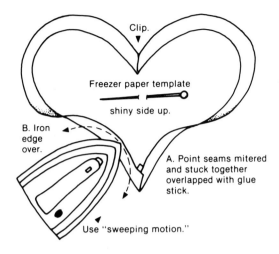

FIGURES 10-7A & 10-7B

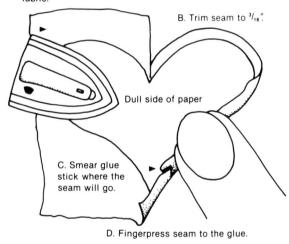

FIGURES 10-8A, 10-8B, 10-8C & 10-8D

resume the sweeping ironing motion to catch the fabric right at the edge and iron it over to the freezer paper.

Note: Some people handle freezer paper in the same manner as Method #5. They leave a biggish clump of fabric which they can pull up and hold while the iron fuses the seam edge. Later they trim back to a neat seam allowance. If you have any trouble, try this.

When the heart is all prepared, iron it in place on the wreath. The exposed shiny center of the freezer paper bastes (fuses) itself to the background cloth. At the same time, its presence protects the top of your appliqué from getting a "seam line" ironed into it. (Another hint from Kate

Fowle: Put a little glue from a glue stick in the middle of the freezer paper's shiny side if you want to "super baste" when you iron it to the background fabric.)

The freezer paper has to be removed. You can pull it out with tweezers just before you complete an appliqué, or you can trim out the back of the appliqué and pull the template out. Some even treat freezer paper as in Method #5. They use it to get the sharply turned edge, then remove the paper before they start to sew.

Some needleartists now do all their appliqué using freezer paper, using it for both thumbnail-size grapes and 6" flowers. "Doesn't it kill you to do all that ironing?" I asked Kate. "I sit and sew and relax in the evening," she replied. "The ironing and any other preparations I do in the day when I am working about the house. Then when I relax to appliqué in the evening, the pre-basted block goes so quickly and easily."

That makes a lot of sense to me. I do the preparation for superfine wreath-stems on the sewing machine. The results are so worthwhile that I don't mind the fact that I'm not sitting and hand-sewing. But I've noticed it's never prepared the same evening that I appliqué. You make yourself a neat "kit" and it's there when you want it, promising you a good time. Think of freezer paper preparation as a gift to yourself. And thank you, Anne Oliver, you've gotten a good thing going.

7. Freezer paper and paste:
Anna Holland is another needle-genius in our area. A gifted artist, she is also a creative technician and came up with a method that has encouraged hundreds of people to make miniature Baltimore-style Album Quilts.

First, iron the freezer paper template to the wrong side of the fabric as in Method #2. Then trim off to a 3/16" seam allowance (Figures 10-8A and 10-8B). Next, smear the exposed, noncoated side of the freezer paper with school paste. Fingerpress your seams to this glue (Figures 10-8C and 10-8D).

Prepare all units to be appliquéd at once, keeping the pieces in an envelope. This method works very well. Those seams can't go anywhere. When you are all finished appliquéing, trim the fabric out to 1/4" seam (or even just a slit) behind the appliqués; if necessary, soak the top to loosen the paste and pull the freezer paper out.

8. [Plastic] template appliqué™:
Rob Benker-Ritchey and Janice Cooke have come up with a new use for modern technology. In their method, the seam is glue-stick-basted to a plastic template left inside the appliqué. Thus prepared,

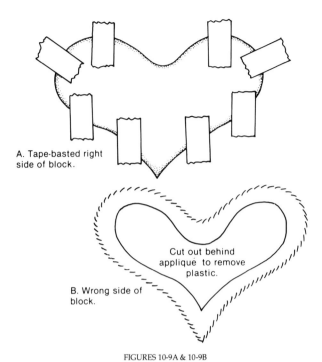

A. Tape-basted right side of block.

Cut out behind appliqué to remove plastic.

B. Wrong side of block.

FIGURES 10-9A & 10-9B

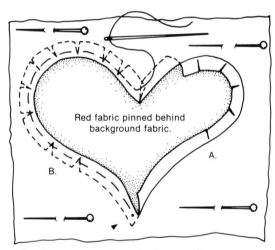

Red fabric pinned behind background fabric.

A.

B.

Basting goes through top (background) fabric, the turned-under seam, and the red fabric pinned beneath.

FIGURES 10-10A & 10-10B

the appliqué is masking-tape-basted to the background fabric (Figure 10-9A).

The extraordinary last step is that you turn the block over and sew from the back, whip-stitching along the edge where you feel the template plastic marking the appliqué's edge. The thread matches the background fabric and your stitches never show on the front. The back is cut out and the template is then removed (Figure 10-9B).

The important implication of this method, to me, is that it allows people to appliqué who would otherwise not be able to: people who are visually impaired can use it, people whose fingers are stiff with arthritis can use a larger needle at no loss with this technique, and impatient twentieth-century children can get quick, good results. And so could any one of us who has ever totally despaired over appliqué.

9. Yo-yo hearts:
Making a yo-yo over a circle template was suggested in the last lesson. You can also make a yo-yo over other simple shapes such as leaves or hearts as well:

Affix a heart cut from a file card (or folder) with a dab of glue stick to the wrong side of your fabric. Trim to 3/16" all around. Take running stitches all the way around, pulling the thread across the "V" of the heart. This looks the same as Figure 10-2, but now there's a paper template inside. When you meet your stitches where they started, tug your thread, gathering the seam around the template like a yo-yo. Tack the thread's end tight, then appliqué to the background. Cut the background fabric to remove the template. Or, simply use your yo-yo heart as an ironing template. Remove it before you sew.

10. Basted reverse (inlaid) appliqué:
This is just as it sounds. The only place where you can do it on this block is the heart just below the one where you started. Baste a 3" square of red behind the heart shape you have drawn on your background fabric. Trim out the center of this heart to 3/16" from the drawn turn line (Figure 10-10A). Clip, as shown, to one to two threads short of the turn line. Push back the seam allowance and baste it under, close to the fold (Figure 10-10B). Appliqué this turned seam. Finish your heart by trimming the red seam allowance back so that it does not show through from under the white seam allowance.

Another pattern for pre-basted appliqué: "Vase of Roses I," Pattern #20. A bold and dramatic pattern, this is a pleasure in basted appliqué.

"Part Two: The Lessons" continues on page 97 following the Color Section.

The Color Section

I. THE LESSON BLOCKS WITH ADDITIONAL ILLUSTRATIVE BLOCKS

The blocks on this page display contemporary fabric use and/or embellishment in classic style. Patterns for these blocks are not included in this book.

1. VASE OF FULL-BLOWN ROSES II. Appliqué by Kate Fowle, 1988. Pattern from *Baltimore Beauties and Beyond, Volumes II* and *III*. (Photo: G. Staley)

2. PATRIOTIC BLOCK. Appliqué by Sylvia Pickell, 1985; quilting by Carol Jo White, 1986-87. Pattern from *Spoken Without a Word*. (Photo: G. Staley)

3. LYRE WITH WREATH AND BIRD. Appliqué by Sylvia Pickell, 1985; quilting by Carol Jo White, 1986-87. Pattern from *Spoken Without a Word*. (Photo: G. Staley)

1

2

3

4

5

6

4. Lesson 1: FLEUR-DE-LIS I (Pattern #1). Elly Sienkiewicz, 1987; quilting by Hazel B. Reed Ferrell, 1988. (Photo: S. Risedorph)

5. Lesson 1: DOUBLE HEARTS (Pattern #2). Jacqueline Janovsky, 1988. (Photo: D. Sienkiewicz)

6. Lesson 2: WREATH OF STRAWBERRY LEAVES (Pattern #22). Jean Stanclift, 1988. (Photo: G. Staley)

7. Lesson 2: YOU ARE PERFECT (Pattern #3). Jacqueline Neeley, 1988. (Photo: G. Staley)

8. Lesson 3: LOVE (Pattern #13). Gene Way, 1988. (Photo: G. Staley)

8

7

9

10

9. Lesson 3: FEATHER-WREATHED HEART (Pattern #14).
Sallye Sileski, 1988. (Photo: G. Staley)

10. Lesson 4: DIVINE GUIDANCE I (Pattern #4). Mary Anne
Johnson, 1988. (Photo: D. Sienkiewicz)

11. Lesson 4: DIVINE GUIDANCE II (Variation of Pattern #4).
Jan Rold, 1988. (Photo: G. Staley)

12. Lesson 4: FEATHERED STAR (Pattern #5). Donna Carman,
1988. (Photo: G. Staley)

13. Lesson 4: STAR OF HEARTS (Pattern #6). Doris Seeley, 1988.
(Photo: D. Sienkiewicz)

11

12

13

14

15

16

17

14. **Lesson 5:** CROSSED LAUREL SPRAYS (Pattern #7). Elly Sienkiewicz, 1986; quilting by Virginia Lemasters, 1988. (Photo: G. Staley)

15. **Lesson 5:** $200,000 TULIPS (Pattern #8). Jane Doak, 1988. (Photo: G. Staley)

16. **Lesson 5:** HOSPITALITY (Pattern #9). Joanne Turnley, 1988. (Photo: G. Staley)

17. **Lesson 5:** MINIATURE BALTIMORE MEDALLION QUILT. Donna Collins, 1987. 14″ x 16″. This quilt illustrates the tiny detail possible with needleturn appliqué. No pattern. (Photo: courtesy of D. Collins)

18. **Lesson 6:** FLEUR-DE-LIS WITH FOLDED ROSEBUDS II (Pattern #10). Elly Sienkiewicz, 1985. (Photo: © G.E. Garrison 1988)

18

19

20

19. Lesson 6: FLEUR-DE-LIS WITH FOLDED ROSEBUDS I. Daphne Hedges, 1984. Pattern from *Spoken Without a Word*. This version is by separate unit appliqué. (Photo: G. Staley)

20. Lesson 6: SWEETHEART ROSE LYRE (Pattern #15). Elly Sienkiewicz, 1988. (Photo: G. Staley)

21. Lesson 6: BRENDA'S ROSEBUD WREATH (Pattern #12). Joanne Turnley, 1988. (Photo: G. Staley)

22. Lesson 7: LYRE WREATH (MARRIAGE) (Pattern #23 for wreath). Joy Nichols, 1988. (Photo: G. Staley)

23. Lesson 7: LYRE WREATH (YEARNING TO BREATH FREE) (Pattern #23 for wreath). Elly Sienkiewicz, 1987. (Photo: S. Risedorph)

21

22

23

24

26

25

24. Lesson 7:
SILHOUETTE WREATH
(Pattern #16).
Elly Sienkiewicz, 1987;
quilting by Hazel B. Reed
Ferrell, 1988. (Photo:
S. Risedorph)

25. Lesson 8:
RUCHED ROSE LYRE (Pattern
#24). Elly Sienkiewicz, 1988.
(Photo: S. Risedorph)

26. Lesson 8:
TOKEN OF GRATITUDE
(Pattern #17).
Dorothy Reise, 1988.
(Photo: G. Staley)

27

28

27. Lesson 9:
CROWN OF LAUREL/BROKEN
WREATH OF CHERRIES
(Pattern #18). Ann Peters,
1988. (Photo: D. Sienkiewicz)

28. Lesson 9:
WREATH OF CHERRIES
(Pattern #11). Roberta Floyd,
1988. (Photo: G. Staley)

29. Lesson 10:
WREATH OF HEARTS II
(Pattern #19).
Elly Sienkiewicz, 1988.
(Photo: G. Staley)

29

30

31

30. Lesson 10:
VASE OF FULL-BLOWN
ROSES I (Pattern #20).
Nonna Crook, 1985. Quilting
by Virginia Lemasters, 1988.
(Photo: S. Sienkiewicz)

31. Lesson 11:
MINIATURE BALTIMORE
ALBUM QUILT.
Darlene Scow, 1987. 30″ x 30″.
Pattern not included. This is
"Beyond Baltimore" by date
and technique; the smallest
of the over 1,000 pieces were
fused for raw-edge buttonholing, the larger pieces were
needleturned for hemmed-
under buttonholing. Made
from patterns by Christine
Bridy and Anna Holland,
this won First Place and
People's Choice Awards in
the Mormon Handicraft
Show, Salt Lake City, 1987.
(Photo: courtesy of D. Scow)

32. Lesson 11:
WREATH AND DOVE
(Pattern #25). Fabric design
and painting by Kate Fowle;
hand buttonhole appliqué
by Stell Lundergan. (Photo:
G. Staley)

32

33

35

33. Lesson 11:
ROSE WREATH WITH RED
BIRDS (Pattern #21).
Mary Lou Fox, 1988. (Photo:
G. Staley)

34. Lesson 12:
RED WOVEN BASKET OF
FLOWERS (Pattern #26).
Cathy Berry, 1988. (Photo:
G. Staley)

35. Lesson 12:
EPERGNE OF FRUIT (Pattern
#27). Cathy Berry, 1988.
(Photo: G. Staley)

34

II. THE GALLERY QUILTS

Detail (Block C-2)

Baltimore and "Beyond": Antique Quilts (Quilts #1 - #4) and Contemporary Quilts (Quilts #5 - #8). Note: Blocks are referred to by letter and number in the text. Blocks run alphabetically from left to right and numerically from top to bottom.

QUILT #1. PIECED AND APPLIQUÉD CLASSIC BALTIMORE ALBUM QUILT.

Signed/dated on the back, *T.A. Hulls, Baltimore, January 1, 1852.* Cross-stitch reads *Baltimore* in the center, and *1776* (the date of the Declaration of Independence, marking the start of the American Revolution) and *A.D. 1784* (the signing of the Treaty of Paris, marking the end of the American Revolution), with homilies around the star. 100" x 100". (Photo: courtesy of Sotheby's Photography Studio)

QUILT #2. CLASSIC BALTIMORE ALBUM QUILT.

Signed *Sarah Pool, Mary J. Pool*, and *Baltimore*; dated circa 1840 in Sotheby's catalog. 106″ x 107⅜″. This quilt sold at auction, January 1987, for a record $176,000 and immediately thereafter was resold by the purchasing dealer for "at least $200,000." (Photo: courtesy of Sotheby's Photography Studio).

As in quilt #1, this quilt reflects the makers' religious devotion and civic and patriotic pride. Both convey a particular life and times. It is this human warmth in addition to their age and beauty which makes these quilts so highly valued.

Detail (Block D-5)

Detail (Block C-4)

QUILT #3. BALTIMORE-STYLE ALBUM QUILT.

From Frederick County (one county away from Baltimore County), Maryland, 1846. Approximately 93" x 93". Collection of Joanna S. Rose. (Photo: courtesy of Joanna S. Rose)

In this rare Jewish Bride's Quilt, block C-4 shows a *chuppah* (wedding canopy) above a table bearing a *kiddush* cup and candles. Other Old Testament symbols include David's Harp, and a dove bearing an olive branch (peace) under an arbor of grapes (for life). These mix with traditionally romantic Bride's Quilt symbols: tulips, strawberries, and the exuberantly stuffed roses from Lesson 7, meaning love. The insignia of personal lives speak to us clearly throughout the Baltimore Album Quilts. These fragile threads stitched in time weave us inseparably into the fabric of all of our lives.

QUILT #4. CLASSIC BALTIMORE ALBUM QUILT. ▶

Multiple signatures, and *Baltimore,...1846* and *1847.*
Approximately 86" x 86". Collection of Lee Porter.
(Photo: G. Staley)

QUILT #5. VICTORIA'S QUILT. ▼

Anna Holland, 1985. Approximately 36" x 36". (Photo:
© 1988 S. Tuttle, courtesy of A. Holland)
    The classic Victorian Album Quilts' colors and airy
set are here taken masterfully "Beyond." The center
is a faithfully reproduced Baltimore Album block
inscribed *And Angels shall watch over thee. Victoria Hope
Dean, April 5, 1985.* Wrapping this blessing as she has
in stars, symbolic of divine guidance, Anna has con-
veyed this exquisite quilt's significance for all time. The
quilt's perfect design is original. The pattern of the
center block is from *Spoken Without a Word.*

Detail (Block C-3)

QUILT #6. THE GOOD LADIES OF BALTIMORE.

Group Quilt, 1984-88. Makers of individual blocks are listed in "Part Three: The Quiltmakers." Border appliquéd by Agnes Cook; quilting by Virginia Lemasters and Carol Jo White. 91″ x 91″. (Photo: © G.E. Garrison 1988)

Fifteen of the blocks in this quilt resulted from the 1984 contest inspired by *Spoken Without a Word*. Elly Sienkiewicz made the other ten blocks and designed the quilt as a Bride's Quilt for her daughter, Katya Sienkiewicz (just ten years old when the quilt was finished).

Detail: FLOWER-WREATHED HEART. The quilt's dedication has been inscribed on this elegant award-winning block by Albertine Veenstra, 1985.

QUILT #7. THE FASCINATING LADIES OF BYGONE BALTIMORE.

Group Quilt, 1984-88. Makers of individual blocks are listed in "Part Three: The Quiltmakers." The border was appliquéd by Zollalee Gaylor, the center medallion by Kathy Pease. Five blocks are from the same contest as quilt #6; seven blocks are by Elly Sienkiewicz who designed and set the quilt. Quilting both designed and sewn by Hazel B. Reed Ferrell. 79″ x 79″. (Photo: S. Risedorph)

   Detail: FLEUR-DE-LIS. The quilt was completed as a "Groom's Quilt" for Donald Sienkiewicz. This block refers to his election in 1987 to the Order of the Arrow, Boy Scouts of America. (Photo: S. Risedorph)

Detail (Block D-4)

Detail (Border)

QUILT #8. FRIENDSHIP'S OFFERING.

Group Quilt, made for Mary Sue Hannan's seventieth birthday, 1986-88. 115″ x 115″. Makers of individual blocks and the quilt's inscription are listed in "Part Three: The Quiltmakers." Center medallion by Kate Fowle; quilted by Emma and Fannie Hershberger, 1988. (Photo: © G.E. Garrison 1988)

Based on the 1847 (Pennsylvania?) quilt made by Sarah Holcomb (pictured in *New Discoveries in American Quilts*, p. 84), this quilt is gloriously "Beyond Baltimore" in color scheme, but otherwise quite close to its classic original. In that quilt, the majority of blocks seem to be paper-cut ones done by cutwork.

Detail: Center border medallion drafted and appliquéd by Jan Sheridan; inscription and calligraphy by Elly Sienkiewicz.

LESSON 11:

Buttonhole Appliqué—Raw-edge Buttonholing, Hemmed-edge Buttonholing, Plus a Modern Buttonholing Miracle

PATTERNS:

"Wreath and Dove," Pattern #25 (Photo 24), and "Rose Wreath with Red Birds," Pattern #21 (Photo 25)

Because classic buttonholing is so time-consuming, this lesson's techniques are taught on a 2" practice heart (for the practice heart pattern, see Figure 11-1). The original Wreath and Dove block (block C-3 in quilt #4) is rare in that it is appliquéd entirely by buttonholing in thread the color of the appliqués. It seems to mark a transitional use of buttonholing in the classic Baltimore Album Quilts. Rose Wreath with Red Birds exemplifies the possibly more typical classic period use of buttonholing as a decorative design accent. The significance of this transition is important to our understanding of these classic quilts.

Is buttonholing back? Not really. Not yet. But I believe we will see more of it as part of the classic Baltimore Album Quilt Revival. There is much more buttonholing in these quilts than we had realized. It seems to be used in the blocks as an embellishment on the occasional motif rather than as a favored means of appliqué.

BUTTONHOLING AS A TRANSITIONAL APPLIQUÉ TECHNIQUE

The *Broderie Perse* and chintz-work quilts[1] were the nineteenth-century's fancy-work quilts before appliquéd Album Quilts became the rage. In the Deep South, they remained the fashion well into the Appliqué Album Quilt period. The primary appliqué stitch in *Broderie Perse* quilts was buttonholing.

In only one block[2] that I have seen in a classic Baltimore Album Quilt was the time-consuming buttonhole stitch used throughout the entire block as the sole appliqué stitch, taken over a raw edge. This block, our lesson's Wreath and Dove, seems to me to have the same pattern drafting, fabric, layout, and inking design-hand as the Metropolitan Museum of Art's classic Album Quilt shown in Photo 26. This quilt is attributed in *Baltimore Album Quilts* to Mary Evans. The Wreath and Dove block from quilt #4, however, seems to be sewn by someone with a uniquely fine nee-

PHOTO 24. "Wreath and Dove," Pattern #25. Buttonhole appliqué and embroidery by Stell Lundergan; fabric selection, painting, and cutting out of appliqués by Kate Fowle; block layout by Jane Doak; pattern drafting and Stell Lundergan's calligraphed signature by Elly Sienkiewicz; 1988. (Photo: G. Staley)

PHOTO 25. "Rose Wreath with Red Birds," Pattern #21. Appliqué, embellishing, fabric placement, and signature by Mary Lou Fox; pattern drafting and fabric selection by Elly Sienkiewicz; 1988. (Photo: G. Staley)

dleartistry, someone who is as much an embroiderer and a "painter with fabric" as a skilled quiltmaker. Furthermore, because this version of the relatively frequent Wreath and Dove block is uniquely buttonholed,[3] it might possibly be a transitional prototype.

PHOTO 26. This quilt is called a "Baltimore Friendship Quilt" by the Metropolitan Museum. Compare the wreath and dove block, F-3, with block C-3 in Lee Porter's quilt #4. *Baltimore Album Quilts* refers to this quilt as "Baltimore Album Quilt, circa 1849, Attributed to Mary Evans." It goes on to say, "A unique feature of this quilt is the handsome design of musical trophies (B-1). Dr. Dunton mentioned, in a notebook, a print-covered pillow belonging to Acsah Goodwin Wilkins whose design depicted a trophy associated in art with the goddess Diana within a circle of morning glories." Compare this block with the block (D-5) in quilt #2 in the Color Section. (Photo: The Metropolitan Museum of Art: The Sansbury-Mills Fund. 1974.24)

FIGURE 11-1

One could hypothesize that a certain very good needleartist designed this block, bypassing the older fashion of white thread and innovatively buttonholing it in *matching* colored thread. She liked the "look" and realized she could achieve virtually the same effect in a fraction of the time by substituting the tiny tack stitch (15-17 stitches per inch[4]) for the minutely close buttonhole stitch (45-47 stitches per inch on this block).

This block would then take one-third the number of stitches, and thus take only one-third the time that it would with the buttonhole appliqué. If one were a professional engaged in production sewing, the time savings would be great, particularly if one added the stack cutting of appliqué shapes discussed in Lesson 8.

Unfortunately, this neat theory doesn't hold water because by 1847, the date inscribed on the Wreath and Dove, there were already dozens of needleturned blocks (in multiple quilts) of the style attributed in *Baltimore Album Quilts* to "Mary Evans." It does, however, underscore the timesavings afforded by the then-current style of needleturning appliqué. And the fact that in the midst of all this ornate, realistically stylized appliqué productivity, some one person chose to appliqué by a method which took three times longer than necessary underscores the probability of multiple appliquérs, one of whom might have been a designer pioneering in this style.

Buttonholing the elaborate Victorian pattern #25 should be worked up to, rather than used as a primer to learn on. Thus we will learn about buttonholing on the Heart Pattern (Figure 11-1). Then you can decide whether to move on to the hemmed-edge buttonhole block, Rose Wreath with Red Birds, or go directly on to the classic challenge, the Wreath and Dove block done over a raw edge.

THE BUTTONHOLE STITCH FOR CLASSIC APPLIQUÉ

1. For raw-edge buttonholing, begin by drawing the heart (from Figure 11-1) onto the right side of your red fabric. This is the drawn seam line, marking where your needle enters the fabric.

2. Cut out this heart, leaving 1/4" seam allowance beyond the drawn line. (Figures 11-2A and 11-2B).

3. Approach the buttonholing as cutwork, trimming back to the true 1/32" seam allowance, about 1 1/2" at a time, just as you are about to sew that section (Figures 11-2C and 11-2D). This means that on a block such as Wreath and Dove, you can baste the whole block out and not worry about fray, because the "true raw edge" won't yet be cut.

4. Baste your buttonhole practice heart to the background fabric.

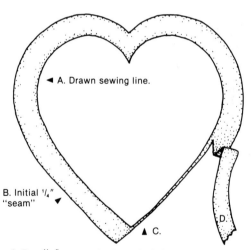

A. Drawn sewing line.
B. Initial 1/4" "seam"
C. True 1/32" seam to be buttonholed over raw edge.
D. Cut back to 1/32" about 1½" at a time.

FIGURES 11-2A, 11-2B, 11-2C, & 11-2D

The thread:
While buttonholing a whole block is rare, the use of colored thread for the decorative accent buttonholing became common in the classic Baltimore Album Quilts. In the Wreath and Dove prototype, a sewing-weight thread in an exact color match to each fabric was used throughout except on the

bow where red was used. This color fact is intriguing in itself: Although matching thread was accessible to the makers of classic quilts, off-white or light-colored thread for tack-stitching remained the norm.

On our heart, we have no choice. These stitches are born to show. Do them in a perfect red thread match for one classic Baltimore Album Quilt look. Or do them in a high-contrast color like white or yellow for another classic look exemplified by the pattern, "Rose Wreath with Red Birds" (Pattern #21) and by the blocks B-1 and C-2 in classic quilt #1.

The buttonhole stitch done over a raw edge:
Use the #11 Sharps appliqué needle. Knot your 18" thread. The basic principle and technique of the buttonhole stitch is to buttonhole towards yourself, with your needle entering on the right through the drawn seam line, and exiting to the left, out the background fabric only, right at the raw edge of the appliqué. Every stitch passes over the tail-end thread of the previous stitch. Right-handed buttonhole moves left to right. Let's go through it step-by-step:

1. To begin the stitch, your needle should enter the background fabric from the back and emerge through the background only, adjacent to the raw edge (Figure 11-3).

2. Push the needle point back into the fabric at the drawn turn line. Without pulling the needle through yet, weave the point under the top and background fabric and have it

emerge through the background only right at the edge of the appliqué, passing over the tail of the previous stitch as it emerges (Figure 11-3).

3. Pull your stitch until that tail-end thread is tucked neatly next to the appliqué's edge. The thread is pulled firmly, but not tightly enough to distort the fabric. Begin again at Step 2, and repeat.

4. Each stitch goes right next to the previous one, or a maximum of one thread-width (one needle's width) apart, giving the Wreath and Dove block 45 to 47 stitches per inch. The combination of the looped thread at the raw edge and the 1/32" "bite" into the fabric make each stitch 1/16" long (Figure 11-4, shown to scale).

Catch fray as you go. Make it lie back down, and sew it flat as though it were integral to the fabric again. Don't clip it or pull it out except if, after you are all finished, you see an occasional recalcitrant thread.

Having a marked "edge" to your design is one of the secrets to very precise, even 1/16" stitches such as those in the photocopied detail of the original block C-3 from quilt #4 (Figure 11-5). As in fine quilting, it is the evenness of length and of distance between the stitches that give the work its beauty. This marked edge can be the line drawn around your template, or it can be the outline of a printed motif cut

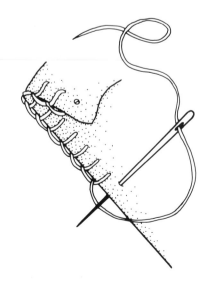

FIGURE 11-3

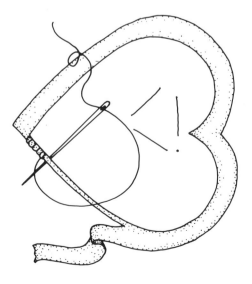

FIGURE 11-4

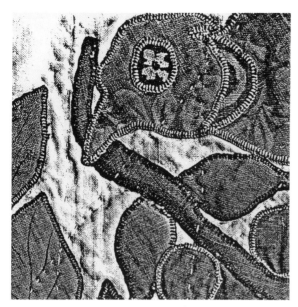

FIGURE 11-5

from another fabric like the butterfly I buttonholed onto the Friendship block from Lesson 10.

The principle of hemmed-edge buttonholing:
First appliqué down a motif, such as the heart, needleturning the 1/8" seam allowance under and tacking it in place. Then buttonhole over this hemmed edge, just as above.

With this method, buttonholing is decorative only—it can be a highly contrasting color, your stitches can be as far apart as you find appealing, and your thread can be decorative as well. Embroidery thread, or crewel wool (black or white) was favored in the classic Baltimore Album Quilts. With practice, you can appliqué the folded seam with just the buttonhole stitch itself, if you choose.

Even with the technical option of wider spacing between stitches, all the buttonholing I've seen in these classic quilts is dense: stitch right next to stitch even in bulky crewel wool on quilt-weight cotton.

There is a surprising amount of this woolwork in these Album Quilts including decorative buttonholing and stem-stitch. Perhaps most astonishing is to see a short, slanted visible tack stitch in thick white crewel wool on leaves. It is the tiny dark green slits of fabric showing between the heavy yarn that look like the serrated edges of those leaves. And undoubtedly, that's the effect intended. The same white wool is heavily buttonholed around the white centers of some stuffed roses as well.

THE MODERN BUTTONHOLING MIRACLE

At 45 to 47 stitches per inch, someone had to think of an easier way. Intentional or not, it was Pellon® that produced a fusible bonding material applicable to hand buttonholing. It carries the felicitous name of Wonder-Under™.

Because this paper-covered bondable fuses the fabric's raw-edge, your stitches can be taken over it and spaced at a relaxing 1/8" apart, reducing the number needed to a more comfortable 16 or so per inch.

The one caveat is that the use of fused buttonholing is ideally confined to a one-layer appliqué. When you layer it, for example in a flower with a circle center, you can see the stiff look that gives the method away. This is only an issue if you want to keep the soft, traditional quilt look.

Darlene Scow's exquisite miniature Appliqué Album Quilt (see Color Plate #31 in the Color Section) has its smallest units fused, then buttonholed. Not only are the stitches fine and even, but the "Beyond Baltimore" color scheme is as fresh and charming as an English garden.

PROCEDURE

Wonder-Under™ is a fusible webbing with a see-through peel-off paper protection. This characteristic makes it much easier to use than earlier fusibles. Here's the best way to fully utilize this wonderful resource:

1. You can easily trace a design onto the paper covering, cut out the shape, iron it onto the back of your appliqué fabric, and finally cut this fusible-backed shape out of your cloth. Peel off the paper backing and your appliqué fabric motif becomes exactly like the "iron-on patches" already familiar to you.

2. Position the motifs on your background fabric.

3. Fuse all your shapes down with a hot dry iron.

4. Now you are ready to buttonhole. I prefer slightly heavier thread for the wider spaced stitches. I generally select the soft, 100% cotton, nonwaxed Molynecke® quilting thread.

Words of encouragement:
Buttonholing, like all stitchery, improves rapidly with practice. Drawing the appliqué's edge (so that you can cut 1/32" beyond it) is a preparation step which will eventually be replaced by a practiced eye and a well-disciplined hand.

There is no evidence that the sewing edge was marked in the classic Wreath and Dove. In fact, the shapes are a bit fat as though the same template was used to cut them as would have been used for appliqués meant to be hemmed under 1/8" to

1/16".[5] This means our buttonholed wreath is simply chubbier, less airy than the similar wreath in the Metropolitan's quilt, pictured in this lesson (block F-3 in Photo 26).

Marking the edge, like cutworking the seam, simply makes it easier for us to do fine buttonholing. A delightful and considerably simpler block with which to make your first forays into buttonholedom is Rose Wreath with Red Birds. It has a small amount of decorative-only buttonholing over a hemmed edge.

NOTES

[1] I am defining chintz-work as chintz print cut-outs seamed under and appliquéd down with a tack or blind stitch. I understand *Broderie Perse* ("Persian Embroidery") to be different from chintz-work in that the appliqué is done with a decorative stitch (buttonholing over a raw edge) and, in addition, embellishing embroidery is done within these appliqués themselves. It is thus a significantly more time-consuming fancywork than chintz-work. In *Broderie Perse*, more buttonhole and other stitches are done atop elements of the print to enrich them. This embroidery seems traditionally to have been done in the same heavier off-white thread of the buttonhole appliqué itself.

We see chintz-work on a minor scale in these classic appliqué Album Quilts (see quilts #1 and #4). Sometimes whole blocks are done in motifs cut from a chintz print and tack-stitched down. Sometimes just a flower or two is used in an appliqué block or fashioned into a bow. Chintz-work of any form is relatively infrequent in these classic Baltimore Album Quilts. The women who made these quilts were on to something new.

To begin with, the good needlewomen of Baltimore were savoring the challenge of creating "from scratch" that realistic floral representation which earlier had been sought from chintz prints. The exotic birds from elegant prints, previously the fashion, were now wrought in layered appliqué by the needleartist herself. It seems to be to these motifs, not to the tack-stitched vestiges of chintz-work, that our fascinating Ladies of Bygone Baltimore added their refined, painstaking buttonhole stitch.

2 Wreath and Dove, center block (C-3) of signed appliqué Album Quilt with "Baltimore," "1846," and "1847," quilt #4, collection of Lee Porter. This block is inscribed "Elizabeth Peters 1847." The copperplate script is done in ink which has bled. This is interesting to note, for none of the elegant inking of leaves or rose hairs on this same block has bled. It is as though the latter were done by one much more skilled in using ink on cloth and the signing done by another.

[3] This Wreath and Dove block (C-3 in quilt #4) seems rare in that the buttonhole stitch is the only appliqué stitch used, and in the fact that the buttonholed thread matches each color fabric perfectly. The only exception to this matching is an artistic one: the brown-hued bow

is stitched in the red of the roses. My hypothesis that a characteristic use of buttonholing, embroidery, and/or chintz cut-outs may help trace a particular prototype design-hand(s) is recent. Unfortunately, one has to have either an exceptional photograph or the actual quilt to observe stitches, and I have only just started to look for these stitchery characteristics as an opportunity to see one of these quilts occurs.

I have, however, observed two other blocks with close to the Wreath and Dove's amount of buttonholing. Both these blocks are in quilt #1 and one is shown as a detail of that quilt in the Color Section. While these blocks are almost entirely buttonholed, their stitches are in the off-white style of the earlier nineteenth century. Transitional chintz-work appears in both quilt #1 and quilt #4.

The Wreath and Dove block is also unique, possibly prototypical, in the design itself. Every element in this design, from the dove to the two stylized roses, to the seven different versions of the calyx and rosebud unit, is repeated identically in other blocks of quilts attributed in *Baltimore Album Quilts* to "Mary Evans." The dove's brown flower-printed rainbow fabric appears throughout the Metropolitan Museum of Art's circa 1849 quilt (Photo 26) as well as the similarly ornate Victorian Abby Aldrich Rockefeller Museum's circa 1850 quilt of the style associated with Baltimore, and in the Baltimore Museum's 1849 Baltimore Album Quilt, made for Miss Elizabeth Sliver (catalog #18).

Close versions of this block design, but never this exact block, are seen, in my experience. For example, in the Metropolitan's block (block F-3 in Photo 26), this same shaped dove with berry sprig is in the center of a similar but slightly different wreath. The Metropolitan quilt's wreaths have a smooth, pat design look, as though made from a perfected pattern. Lee Porter's Wreath and Dove has the slightly more hesitant look of a design still being worked out. Awkwardnesses remain in it: the stem that lies atop the cutwork rose, or the one that sticks out from under the bow, not quite hidden by the overlapping leaf.

In the Metropolitan quilt's rose wreaths, the bow/stem issue has been resolved by a fulsome rose. This creates the off-set circle center which by circa 1849-50 seems to me to typify the evolved ornate Victorian-style rose wreath format. This is apparent later than the 1846-47 Wreath and Dove block. One could hypothesize that these elaborate rose wreath designs became popular and that those being repeated had become certain well-balanced copiable "mass-produceable" ones.

My thought is that block C-3 in quilt #4 was either a prototype or a basted-out, already ink-embellished block kit exquisitely sewn by someone who had moved the pieces around a bit while buttonholing it.

[4] This is the number of tack stitches per inch in Currant Wreath and Doves, block B-2 in the same quilt #4, which I believe may also reflect the same fabric and design influence sources as the Wreath and Dove block. I personally believe that the artists who drafted the most elegant realistic Victorian blocks are probably also responsible for the most skillful, pleasing renditions of the simpler one- and two-color designs found in the classic quilts stemming from the Methodist Church. A good example of a quilt which appears to be designed by one skilled hand and which includes both types of blocks is the circa 1850 Baltimore-style one shown in the *Quilt Engagement Calendar Treasury* (p. 148).

Throughout the Baltimore Album Quilts, we see both folk-arty renditions of a given design and very sophisticated versions of the same. The style hallmarks which lead me to connect block B-2 with the best of the design-hands are: an appealing, particularly well-drafted version of this popular wreathed heart design; blue fabric of the heavier weave found in the Album Quilts connected in *Baltimore Album Quilts* to the Methodist quiltmakers (each bird is pieced, twice, and cut from a blue, possibly "rainbow" print); the birds' typically stylized shape; and the "bright eye" of the bird cut from a floral print. Besides the different stitch, the sewing of block B-2 is less skillful than that of the Wreath and Dove block.

[5] This is an intriguing fact. If pattern transfer, typically, was cutting an appliqué motif with tiny seam included, but not marked, then someone receiving (or purchasing) a basted-kit could appliqué it as she chose. Only the differences in her needle-style would, to the knowing eye, distinguish her block from the next: white thread, colored thread; buttonhole, tack, or blind stitch; tiny seam, medium seam; smooth seam, halting seam; stuffed appliqué or flat. It bespeaks many needles, all plying the same path.

Thus, multiple-quiltmakers could account for the phenomenal number of quilts/blocks which appear at first to be designed by one person or persons. Different seam widths used by individual appliquérs could account as well for different "looks" in these quilts, from thin (The John and Rebecca Chamberlain quilt, *Quilter's Newsletter Magazine*, #202), to medium (Baltimore Museum of Art's Elizabeth Sliver quilt, catalog #18), to plump (Lee Porter's buttonholed Wreath and Dove block). It would account as well for the varied quality of the stitching in blocks which might in many other respects be attributable to a common design-hand.

In 1978, Shiela Betterton wrote in *Quilts and Coverlets from the American Museum in Britain* of an exquisite Album Quilt inscribed "Alice A. Ryder, April 1st, 1847, Baltimore, Md." Concerning the eleven realistic Victorian-style blocks (of the sort attributed to Mary Evans in *Baltimore Album Quilts*) Betterton suggested, "Because of the similarity of some of the designs it is possible that some blocks were made from a professionally drawn pattern or were bought in 'kit' form." Jeana Kimball noted that support for this theory comes in Dolores Hinson's discussion of the Julia Thompson quilts in

American Graphic Quilt Designs (pp. 221-39). Several of the block styles attributed in *Baltimore Album Quilts* to Mary Evans appear to be pictured there in a quilt which family history says was made entirely by Julia Thompson, herself.

For an example of this varied stitching, look closely at Photo 6, using a magnifying glass. While the decorative realism of this Victorian design has been superbly drafted in a now-familiar style, the appliqué is not well done. See, for example, the layered rose to the left of the flag. Its petals and center are awkwardly placed and their curves are bumpy in contrast to the smooth fluid appliquéd lines of the rose sprig in Photo 18. The inking of the block pictured in Photo 6, however, is as nicely done as any. Might this block have been a basted-out "kit" with the inking already on the background?

If one accepts the multiple seamstresses theory, block/quilt kits could have been made on speculation or on commission. They could have been purchased as kits, ready-made blocks, customized tops or top kits, and possibly even as completed quilts, as has been suggested. Furthermore, multiple quilts seem to have been made or at least designed by just one maker. Differing style variations within the decorative realistic Victorian style suggest to me more than one quiltmaker designing the whole quilt herself.

Could we gain any insight into the possible commercial aspect of these classic quilts by thinking about how quilts today are made? Most quilts today are made primarily for keeping or as gifts beyond price, made out of love or affection and without profit-making intent. Many a quilter has said, "I'd give one of my quilts away, but I wouldn't sell it." The quilting itself is commissioned with some frequency, but at a fee for service which by all reckonings is low for the amount of time put in. Rarely can appliqué be commissioned and seldom is the designer of the quilt separate from its maker, except in group quilts. Group quilts are at such an advantage in the sharing of financial resources, talents, and time, that they are judged separately in all respects. The only possible disadvantage in a voluntary group quilt is the unevenness of the needleworkers' skill. Because the investment is shared and largely donated, group quilts are the most popular form of fundraising quilt.

All this is familiar to us as quiltmakers. What may be more difficult for a nonquilter to understand are the monuments to generosity and affection which quilters in groups can construct. Anyone who has worked on a group quilt, such as the Friendship's Offering quilt made for Sue Hannan (quilt #8), has shared this pleasure. Perhaps, similarly, the early Baltimore Album Quilts were made as gifts without profit-making (even to the church) motive. That fundraising schemes for the church, or business for seamstresses, then presented themselves after this "artistic entity" had evolved a bit, seems quite possible. This commercial aspect has been variously suggested.

The intense closeness of community through which these quilts were made is clear. That some in this community should cooperate to make blocks which carried names of others (the men, for example) who perhaps paid for materials and services (appliqué, quilting, binding) is within our own experience as quilters. Again, consider quilt #8, Friendship's Offering. Ruth Stonely, too far away in Australia to sew, contributed financially. Betty Nock, in Washington, doesn't sew but did contribute the complicated bookkeeping and eloquent recordkeeping. Both these women were as much a part of the group as those who organized, designed, and sewed, and so their names are inscribed on that quilt. The group's financial contributions enabled us to have the quilt professionally quilted. So, too, authors Katzenberg, Dunton, Bourdes, Wright, and the Orlofskys suggest professional seamstress help in the Baltimore Album Quilts.

Parallels between our modern group quilts and those of the nineteenth-century are interesting and may in part support theories originally proposed in *Old Quilts*. But the dramatic stylistic differences which sets these Baltimore Albums apart from other Album Quilts (and their great numbers) remain a puzzle. Clearly, many many women were being influenced by the same design sources and were sharing, initially at least, the same fabric choices. This reinforces the speculation that the *group* and its dynamics were a fundamental influence in the ornate Victorian style associated with mid-nineteenth-century Baltimore.

Dena Katzenberg connects such a group with the Methodists and identifies them as possibly called the "Ladies of Baltimore." These church women's lives were probably linked closely to circles of other women in the community through associations reflected in these classic quilts: women whose husbands were in fraternal lodges together, or whose paths crossed through benevolent societies, or commercial, political, military, or civic groups. Whatever the catalyst, great numbers of Baltimore women were inspired to prodigious levels of quiltmaking which in turn reflected common threads.

That the frontier-breaking, more realistic Victorian style would be imitated in its own time seems inevitable. Album Quilts, then as now, seem to have evolved from mixed-block group quilts to quilts designed by one person. We see this same progression today. As you participate in a group Album Quilt, the ambition grows insistent to make one all your own where you can impose a consistent style and fabric palette.

Thus, the style identified previously as "Mary Evans" may, in fact, entail more than one person. The phenomenal number of quilts reflecting the decorative Victorian realism associated in *Baltimore Album Quilts* with "Mary Evans" bespeaks many many quiltmakers participating in a community probably familiar in many respects to us all. We know that some of us are relentlessly creative, while others of us are superb copiers. We know the extent of time, trouble, and expense we will go to to view a fabulous quilt, obtain a special fabric, learn someone's special technique. We know how closely quilt fashions and quiltmaking methods are tied together across the country and abroad.

In a bustling seaport hub, might not many elements of the same phenomenon have been going on in and around mid-nineteenth-century Baltimore? My feeling is that in the multitude of "Mary Evans' " quilts and blocks (well over one hundred, by some counts), we may be seeing not only multiple individuals doing the sewing, but also more than one very talented needle-artist doing the most outstanding designing.

LESSON 12:

The "Mary Evans" Challenge

PATTERNS:
"Red Woven Basket of Flowers," Pattern #26 (Photo 27), and "Epergne of Fruit," Pattern #27 (Photo 28)

BON VOYAGE

This really is the last stop on this part of our journey together. Here, two more classic blocks are given, but with no additional instructions. You already know more than enough to tackle these enjoyably—and successfully. Instead of instructions, these blocks come to you with "The 'Mary Evans' Challenge."

In replicating them, using the processes developed so long ago, you will be carrying on a tradition, perpetuating our heritage. Moreover, you will literally be reenacting, to some extent, the social role of making a classic Baltimore Album Quilt. By understanding what making an ornate, more realistic-style block means to you now, you gain insight into what this might have meant then. Meaning is the most fragile part of classic quilts. We can *see* the physical aspects of these masterpieces of our heritage—they still warm and beautify our lives. But they hint at so much more, so much significance "spoken without words" (Photos 29 and 30).

As a quiltmaker, you are a folklorist, preserving techniques and patterns of our physical heritage, but also passing on understandings of the social role quiltmaking plays. You know why you quilt, what you want to convey through each quilt. I hope you will share any understandings this gives you into our classic quilts. I hope you will write at least a few words about each quilt's significance, perhaps on its label, for future ages will wonder at it.

Sharing from my own work on appliqué Album Quilts, it seems apparent to me that Mary Evans, or any one person, could not, in a six-year period,[1] have made the now dozens of quilts popularly attributed to her, alone. The time simply isn't there. Just appliqué hours themselves, on an ornate, more realistic, Victorian-style pattern such as those in this lesson, run about forty to sixty hours.[2]

Keeping diligently at it, this would be about a block per long workweek. At an average of 25 blocks per quilt, with an intricate appliqué border equaling another 20 to 25 blocks (plus design re-

PHOTO 27. "Red Woven Basket of Flowers," Pattern #26. Appliqué, fabric selection and use, embellishing, and backstitched signature by Cathy Berry; fabric selection and pattern drafting by Elly Sienkiewicz; 1988. (Photo: G. Staley)

PHOTO 28. "Epergne of Fruit," Pattern #27. Appliqué, fabric selection and use, embellishing, and back-stitched signature by Cathy Berry; fabric selection and pattern drafting by Elly Sienkiewicz; 1988. (Photo: G. Staley)

search and drafting, fabric acquisition, selection, template-making, cutting, basting, then setting-out, basting, quilting and binding—and never working on Sundays), Mary Evans by herself might have made six quilts total, a quilt a year for the six years in which work attributed to her appears.

I share these thoughts hoping to generate a brisk, open exchange of ideas. The work today, both in replicating antique designs and in innovative designing in the Classic Style, is nothing short of astounding. Current quiltmaking's remarkable quality has implications for our understanding of the past. Was "Mary Evans," as we know her by an identifiable design style, just one person? Or do we in fact see the interaction of several exceptionally talented needleartists at work?

We know the impact of masterpiece quiltmaking among ourselves: a seminal quilt is published and many by other hands soon rival it. Was it ever thus? We quiltmakers make and share, borrow ideas and fabrics, and grow. We come from a proud tradition and the better we understand ourselves, the better able we are to understand our classic past.

This lesson's challenge is more than a challenge to execute these complicated patterns successfully, though that is accomplishment enough. It is also an exhortation to have the courage of your own inner vision in your needleart, rather than being overly concerned about somebody else's rules. Masterpieces like the classic Baltimore Album Quilts come from people who have the courage of their own convictions.

Think about it. If you have technical perfection only, you have an incredible talent. You can recreate masterpieces and keep valuable knowledge about our culture alive. You pay homage to existing beauty, and make it your own. Moreover, you know the details of its making with an intimacy that scholars can only guess at. The accomplishment and rewards of technical perfection are deservedly admired.

If, beyond technical perfection you have a good color sense, or a genius for fabric choice, then you add to the heirloom masterpiece in a way that makes it more your own. To add even a small something that is just you carries a classic masterpiece into the present— and "Beyond."

The classic Baltimore Album Quilts were marvels in their own time and they are marvels today. A simple yardstick of this is the fact that Baltimore Album Quilts have recently sold for the price of a very nice house, more than any other quilts have ever sold for.[3] To us as quiltmakers, though, they carry a far more important message: "Be yourself."

For we see in these record-price quilts, fabric use which contradicts the rules contemporary "authorities" give us: heavy velvet mixed with cotton on small motifs, heavier cottons hand-appliquéd, thick crewel wool buttonholed over light cotton, and white thread used to appliqué every color of fabric imaginable. Green leaves, uncut-out, show through "Mary Evans'" white silk roses (Photo 18)—which are nonetheless lovely for it.

PHOTO 29. This block (C-1 from quilt #2 in the Color Section) shows a stately—though unidentified—Maryland House, and successfully conveys to us particular lives and times. (Photo: Sotheby's Photography Studio)

PHOTO 30. This block (C-5 from quilt #2 in the Color Section) shows what appears to be a statehouse. Might this be our nation's Capitol before its new dome was added during the Civil War? It may be the Charles Bullfinch dome, which from the east front gave the Capitol this look from 1825-56. The block's designer may have wanted to honor Bullfinch, who died in 1844, or the Capitol as she knew it. Further research into this quilt's picture blocks may focus its date a bit better. For example, block A-3 appears to be a reference to William Henry Harrison's 1840 "Log cabin and hard cider" presidential campaign, while block E-3 looks like the new dome and wing units chosen by contest in 1850 to enlarge the Capitol. (Photo: Sotheby's Photography Studio)

PHOTO 31. "Immigrant Influences: Album of Heritage," 72" x 72,"1985-86. Sylvia Pickell made this impressive contemporary quilt in classic Baltimore Album Quilt-style to honor the Statue of Liberty on its centennial. Expressing herself fluently in this classic appliqué style, Sylvia seems to feel a kinship with the Baltimore quiltmakers of yore, saying, "If the Statue of Liberty had existed back then, I'm sure it would have been the first thing the Ladies of Baltimore would have put in their quilts!" She did extensive research, drafted all the blocks (which are her original designs), appliquéd, ink-and-thread embellished, quilted, and bound this elegant masterpiece at a relentless pace to enter it in the Museum of American Folk Art's "Great American Quilt Contest" of 1986. As in so many classic Album Quilts, the maker's deep love for her country and an appreciation of its history are readily apparent. (Photo: S. Pickell)

We see there both technically perfect repetition of patterns and awkward imitations of recognizable designs. We see ornate, realistic, Victorian-style blocks stitched both exquisitely and less finely. What we see most, though, is exuberant creativity: needlewomen being themselves. This is the heart of why Baltimore Album Quilts stand out among Album Quilts, then as now.

When good technique is wedded to a strong sense of "how I like it," modern masterpieces to enrich our culture are made. I can't think of a better quilt to exercise your taste on than the classic Baltimore Album Quilt style. By its very nature you are asked to make so many choices in fabric, color, block design, sets, and borders, that you *have* to be yourself. Many will go further, and add to this a penchant for symbolism and a desire to depict the evidence of a life and times. And among us there will also be not just one, but a small handful of "Mary Evanses" with such strong inner voices and such expressive talents that they will sing out through contemporary Albums as hers does from the classic ones of old.

NOTES

[1] *Baltimore Album Quilts*, p.14.

[2] My time ran about 50 hours, Donna Collins reported 40 hours, Sylvia Pickell, 50 hours, Cathy Berry, 40 to 60 hours. Sylvia kept a log, clocking the hours she put in on "Immigrant Influences—Album of Heritage" (Photo 31). There were 896 hand-work hours plus 200 design research/drawing hours. This 1,096 hours (the equivalent of 27 40-hour work weeks) went into making a 72" square quilt: a quilt a bit less than *half* the square footage of the Baltimore Museum of Art's Classic Baltimore Album Quilt (104" x 104") inscribed "To Miss Elizabeth Sliver" and attributed in its catalog to Mary Evans. Thus, even if that classic quilt didn't quite take twice the time to make that Sylvia's did, it would have taken one woman roughly a year of 40-hour weeks to make, or one quilt a year. She could reasonably have made no more than six quilts in the period from 1846-52.

[3] See quilt #2 which sold initially at Sotheby's for a record $176,000. It then immediately resold for "at least $200,000" confirmed the dealer. See also the John and Rebecca Chamberlain Baltimore Album Quilt on the cover of *Quilter's Newsletter Magazine*, #202, which sold at Sotheby's for $110,000 (including the auction house surcharge) in January 1988.

Part Three: The Quiltmakers:

About the Needleartists Whose Work Appears in *Baltimore Beauties and Beyond.*

A contest was held in 1984 asking entrants to reproduce, or base a block on, a design from the book *Spoken Without a Word*. There were ten winners. These contest winners were the inspiration for this book. Their enthusiasm and generosity have been essential to both the quilts which they helped make, and to *Baltimore Beauties and Beyond*. These latter-day good "Ladies of Baltimore" were later joined by other needleartists, including master quilters. Additional artists appear with their work in *Volumes II* and *III*. These women, every one, have my profound gratitude.

THE CONTEST WINNERS

Winning blocks, plus further contributions to this book, are noted. Winners appear in alphabetical order. For brevity, throughout this section, I've referred to quilt #6, "The Good Ladies of Baltimore," as "Ladies of Baltimore." Similarly, quilt #7, "The Fascinating Ladies of Bygone Baltimore," is here just "Fascinating Ladies."

JEANNE BENSON, Adelphi, Maryland: Victorian Grapevine Wreath, block C-1 in quilt #7 ("Fascinating Ladies").

Trained in studio art, Jeanne is a designer, quiltmaker, and teacher. Her work has been chosen for national exhibition including the State Department's "Art in Embassies" program.

AGNES COOK, Silver Springs, Florida: Hunting Scene in "More Maryland Flowers" in *Volume II*; Circle of Hearts, block C-5 in quilt #6 ("Ladies of Baltimore"); plus that quilt's entire Bow and Hammock border.

Agnes started quilting in 1974. Her first two quilts were a king-size Cathedral Window, and a trapuntoed Star of the Bluegrass. She soon began entering national contests. She reports that appliquéing the Baltimore Album Quilt border was both a challenge and a joy.

NONNA CROOK, Gallup, New Mexico: Trumpet Vine, block E-5; Christmas Cactus, block A-5; and Vase of Roses I, block B-1, all in quilt #6 ("Ladies of Baltimore").

Wife, mother of "two super little boys," O.B. nurse, anthropology student, and designer in stained glass and fabric, Nonna writes, "My success with challenging blocks is a matter of attitude. One step at a time, and before I know it, the block is finished."

JUNE DIXON, Arthur, Illinois: Heart Wreath of Flowers (June's original design), block A-3 in quilt #7 ("Fascinating Ladies"); and Friendship's Offering, block D-2 in quilt #6 ("Ladies of Baltimore").

June was taught to sew at nine by her mother who said, "Anything worth doing is worth doing right." Trained in art, and well-versed in all the needlearts, June is an active quilting guild member and has won numerous national contests.

ZOLLALEE AMOS GAYLOR, Midwest City, Oklahoma: Grapevine Wreath, block E-2, and Strawberry Wreath, block E-3, both in quilt #6 ("Ladies of Baltimore"); and the entire Peony and Hammock border of quilt #7 ("Fascinating Ladies").

"Mother believed that a woman should know how to sew a fine seam," Zollalee writes. "To this end, she gave me my first thimble when I was five and set me to piecing four-patch blocks. My mother quilted until she was 84. I pray I can last at least that long."

DAPHNE HEDGES, Columbia, Missouri: Acanthus Leaves in "More Maryland Flowers" (*Vol. II*); and Fleur-de-Lis and Rosebuds I in the Lesson Blocks.

Daphne has been quilting for about ten years and has made six other Christmas quilts. It was perhaps inevitable that she wouldn't stop until she had a Baltimore-style Christmas quilt. She also has been working in Amish style, miniatures, and scrap quilts.

ELOISE LEWIS MCCARTNEY, Youngstown, Ohio: Washington Monument in Baltimore in "More Maryland Flowers" (*Vol. II*); and Flower Basket (Eloise's original design), block E-4 in quilt #6 ("Ladies of Baltimore").

Professionally a secondary-school Spanish teacher, Eloise was inspired by the quilts of her grandmother and took up quilting in the early 1980s. In her enthusiasm, she has entered and won many national contests.

SYLVIA PICKELL, Sumter, South Carolina: Pineapple Block; Star with Currants, block A-2; Patriotic Block, block B-4; Hunting Scene, block D-3; and Lyre with Wreath and Bird, block D-4 in quilt #6 ("Ladies of Baltimore").

Sylvia's much-published Baltimore Album-style quilt, "Immigrant Influences: Album of Heritage," reflects tremendous research, understanding, originality, and artistry. Having won many prizes with intricate handwork, contemporary quick-pieced quilts are Sylvia's current pursuit.

MARY TODA, Girard, Ohio: Rose of Sharon Wreath, block A-4 in quilt #6 ("Ladies of Baltimore") and

Crossed Trumpet Vines (original design), block C-4 in quilt #7 ("Fascinating Ladies").

Relatively new (1984) to quilting, Mary is a teacher of geometry who prefers designing geometric patchwork and symmetrical appliqué designs. "I just love quiltmaking," she says, echoing us all.

ALBERTINE VEENSTRA, Acton, Massachusetts: Parasol; two Roses and Climber blocks, A-1 and D-1, in quilt #7 ("Fascinating Ladies"), all Albertine's original designs; plus Flower-Wreathed Heart, block C-3 in quilt #6 ("Ladies of Baltimore").

Professionally trained as a seamstress, Albertine worked in the garment industry in Brussels, then came to the United States. "I fell in love with American quilting, especially with appliqué. My grandmother taught me to sew originally, admonishing, 'Don't waste the Lord's good time.' " Albertine teaches quiltmaking professionally and also restores antique quilts.

RECENT MEMBERS OF THE GOOD LADIES OF BALTIMORE

Blocks appear in the Lesson Blocks color plates (the Color Section), unless otherwise noted. Quiltmakers are listed alphabetically. Contributing needleartists who have made blocks not shown in this volume will be introduced with their work in Volumes II and III of *Baltimore Beauties*.

CATHERINE A. BERRY, North Quincy, Massachusetts: Epergne of Fruit, and Red Woven Basket of Flowers.

"I have found quilting, which I began about three years ago, to be the most satisfying craft I have ever endeavored. For me, appliqué is the finest needleart form." Cathy has a young family, works at Tumbleweeds Quilting Shop, is an active member of Rising Star Quilters, and teaches quiltmaking.

DONNA CARMAN, Boulder, Colorado: Feathered Star.

Fairly new to quilting, Donna is a member of the Colorado Quilting Council. Renowned for her precise and beautiful quilting, Donna is prolific in her quiltmaking which includes work in miniatures as well.

DONNA COLLINS, Bridgeport, New York: "Miniature Baltimore Medallion Quilt."

Begun only three years ago, Donna's quilt productivity is prodigious. After making seventeen full-size quilts, she completed ten more from miniature to double-bed size. Donna makes dolls and miniature quilts professionally, works full-time, teaches quilting, and markets patterns for her miniatures. She shares this hint: "I used threads pulled from the fabric to appliqué with. This makes for small threads, but it is worth it for the perfect match."

JANE DOAK, Boulder, Colorado: $200,000 Tulips.

Trained as a commercial artist, Jane now lends her talent to quiltmaking and the Colorado Quilting Council. Expert at embroidery and appliqué, she and her mother, Stell Lundergan, recreated the famous nineteenth-century New York "Bird of Paradise" appliqué Album Bride's Coverlet Quilt. As generous as talented, Jane designed and donated a magnificent set of seasonal banners to her church. Her work hung in 1988 in the Pioneer Museum, Colorado Springs.

HAZEL B. REED FERRELL, Middlebourne, West Virginia: Original designing and quilting of "The Fascinating Ladies of Bygone Baltimore."

Wife, mother, and grandmother, Hazel has been designing, quilting, and finishing quilts for 35 years. Her talent has won Hazel's quilts numerous prizes and blue ribbons, plus inclusion in three museum collections in this country. She was the state winner for West Virginia in the Great American Quilt Contest. She writes, "My quilting ideas are taken from nature and done freehand."

ROBERTA FLOYD, Pasadena, Maryland: Wreath of Cherries.

Roberta writes, "I played under my grandmother's quilt frame and pulled batting from the quilts therein. Later I quilted with my mother and husband, and in 1975, as our local libraries began to make bicentennial quilts, I took quilting very seriously. I have taught quilting, and won my share of awards, but I quilt for the sheer joy of creating a work of art."

KATHARINE KENT IVISON FOWLE, Washington, D.C.: Vase of Full Blown Roses II; designer/fabric painter of Wreath and Dove II block; and designer (with Elly Sienkiewicz) of quilt #8, "Friendship's Offering."

Needlework skill, an eye for fine reproduction, a love of folk art, a unique technical creativity and talent, coupled with enviable energy make Kate a prolific needleartist. Her works are pieced, painted, and appliquéd. She teaches stenciling and appliqué on Martha's Vineyard as well as in Washington, D.C.

MARY LOU FOX, Mount Pleasant, Michigan: Rose Wreath with Red Birds.

Mary Lou writes, "I am an avid quilter and cross-stitcher, presently working on a Baltimore Bride's Album and a Folk Art appliqué quilt. I have four teenagers and a husband and a full-time job, but manage to stitch almost every day." Mary Lou's block attests to her superb needleartistry.

ANNA HOLLAND, Waterford, Virginia: "Victoria's Quilt" (quilt #5).

Anna is twice-published and a blue-ribbon winner many times over; her captivating quilt-art reflects her art background. One of the first to miniaturize Baltimore Album Quilts, she made "Mini-Madness I" of antique cloth. She is generously active in area quiltmaking: she headed the Waterford Appliqué Album Quilt, teaches, markets her miniature pattern, and trades stitching time with other professionals.

JACKIE JANOVSKY, Annapolis, Maryland: Double Hearts.

"My love for needlework has lead me to teach smocking, French handsewing, doll construction, and quilting techniques at our local quilt store." Jackie has made a prize-winning appliqué quilt, a block for Leslie Greenberg's Sunbonnet quilt, and designs for Susan McKelvey's pattern series.

MARY ANNE JOHNSON, Boulder, Colorado: Divine Guidance.

Mary Anne teaches quilting, makes dolls and other wonderfully creative boutique items, and is an award-winning quiltmaker of noteworthy industry and talent. An active member of the booming Colorado Quilting Council, she sews regularly with a small group of eight friends, "The L and H Quilters."

JEANA KIMBALL, Kearns, Utah: Guardian Angels, block B-2 in "The Good Ladies of Baltimore."

A talented needleartist ("Roman Coins," Quilt Art '86; "Blueberry Harvest," American Quilter), Jeana's love is appliqué. Her original Baltimore-style Album Quilt designs are the focus of her book, Reflections on Baltimore. Commenting on the wealth of design possibilities within the classic Album Quilt style, Jeanna observed, "We look at the same quilts and see different things."

VIRGINIA LEMASTERS, Marietta, Ohio: Co-quilter of "The Good Ladies of Baltimore" (quilt #6).

Raised in a rural area of the Appalachian foothills, Virginia began quilting at age 13 as a necessity. Now 72, and a widow, she has developed a love for it and a discipline which has become a fine art. Over 800 quilts in this country bear her handiwork. She works long hours at the quilting frame, where she is happiest.

STELL LUNDERGAN, Chesterfield, Missouri: Hand buttonholing of Wreath and Dove.

A master quiltmaker, Stell's pleasure is in executing the finest of hand needlework. With help from her daughter, Jane Doak, Stell faithfully reproduced the brilliant New York 1858-63 "Bird of Paradise" appliqué Album Bride's Coverlet. It is a breathtaking tour de force of appliqué. Her exquisite buttonholing on the Wreath and Dove block is unparallelled.

JACKIE NEELEY, Oak Park, Illinois: You Are Perfect.

Jackie learned needlework at her grandmother's knee. Her love of quiltmaking has taken her to workshops, lectures, and symposia across the country. As well as being a productive quiltmaker, she enjoys learning about all aspects of the subject and is an active member of the Illinois Quilters' Guild.

JOY NICHOLS, Portland, Oregon: Marriage Block.

A professional seamstress, Joy delights and excels in all forms of needlework, from precision machine piecing to embroidered embellishment of hand appliqué. Joy shares her talent and enthusiasm by teaching. More of her ingenious fabric usage and splendid original designs appear in subsequent volumes.

BRENDA PAPADAKIS, Indianapolis, Indiana: Original design of Brenda's Rosebud Wreath.

A math teacher, Brenda writes, "I'm a sentimentalist, always feeling emotional attachment to past quilters. When I'm strip piecing, I'm reminded of the hours they spent years ago on these same traditional patterns, moments stolen from their daily chores. Yet, it is appliqué that turns my thoughts from their labor to 'matters of the heart,' the silent sharing of their souls."

KATHY PEASE, Mount Pleasant, Michigan: Peony Medallion Center (blocks B-2, B-3, C-2, and C-3) in quilt #7 ("Fascinating Ladies").

Kathy is a productive appliqué artist of exceptional skill. Mother of a young family, she still manages to attend quilting seminars and to generously volunteer her talents to national quiltmaking projects. Her needlework graces several quilting books in addition to this one.

THEODOSIA ANN PETERS, Mount Pleasant, Michigan: Cherry Garland/Crown of Laurel.

Raised in the home of a quilter, Ann herself discovered the joy in this needleart in 1980. Now, with six children, she attends university part-time, substitute teaches, reads, hunts, and teaches quilting. "I enjoy most every aspect of quilting except finishing the project. For I feel I've said good-bye to a friend and companion."

DOT REISE, Severna Park, Maryland: Token of Gratitude.

This block represents one of Dot's first appliqué pieces. A meticulous needleartist, Dot drew on her art training, imitating nature by tightening the center circles on the white rose. She suggests careful thought as to sequence in making this block. Long interested in Baltimore Albums, Dot anticipates making one for herself.

JAN ROLD, Longmont, Colorado: Divine Guidance II.

An enthusiastic member of the Colorado Quilting Council, Jan has served on the board and is currently membership chair. Mother of three young children, she began quiltmaking about ten years ago. Her inspiration was receiving a Marriage Quilt made by her grandmother.

DARLENE SCOW, Salt Lake City, Utah: "Miniature Baltimore Album Quilt."

Winner of the Best of Show award in the Mountain Mist '83 Contest, Darlene writes, "I worked many years as a dressmaker. I've been quilting about ten years, I like to do needlepoint and cross-stitch also. I like appliqué work the best, but any kind of quilting is wonderful."

DORIS SEELEY, Boulder, Colorado: Star of Hearts.

Doris is immersed in the needlearts she loves. She served a record three years as president of the 700-member Colorado Quilting Council and participates in a special appliqué guild, plus the Friends of Counted Embroidery. Since she started quiltmaking in 1979, she has both taught quiltmaking and attended every national symposium possible.

ELLY SIENKIEWICZ, Washington, D. C.: Design (with Kate Fowle) of quilt #8; design and set of quilt #6, plus its blocks: Crossed Laurel Sprays, A-1; Fleur-de-Lis with Folded Rosebuds II, A-3; Hunting Scene, B-3; Red Vases, Red Flowers (inlaid appliqué), B-5; Wreathed Heart, C-1; Katya and Her Cats (Elly's original design), C-2; S. & E. Sienkiewicz at Home (Elly's original design), C-4;

Asymmetrical Rose Sprays, D-1; Hearts and Tulips, D-5; and Acanthus, E-1; and design and set of "Ladies of Baltimore" (quilt #6).

Design and set of quilt #7 ("Fascinating Ladies") plus its blocks: Silhouette Wreath (Elly's original design), A-2; Fleur-de-Lis I, A-4; Yearning To Breathe Free (Elly's original design), B-1; Rose of Sharon, B-4; Fancy Flowers I, D-2; Wreathed Heart, D-3; and Fleur-de-Lis II, D-4.

Lesson Blocks: Fleur-de-Lis I, Crossed Laurel Sprays, Fleur-de-Lis with Folded Roses II, Sweetheart Rose Lyre, Lyre Wreath: Yearning to Breathe Free, Ruched Rose Lyre, and Wreath of Hearts.

Daughter of an artist who loves needlework, Elly has sewn since childhood. Appliqué and embroidery were her first needlework loves and were incorporated when she began quiltmaking in 1974. Originally a high school history and English teacher, Elly has been professionally involved in quiltmaking for 15 years.

SALLYE SILESKI, Severna Park, Maryland: Feathered Wreath.

Trained in commercial art, Sallye began quiltmaking for the Bicentennial in 1974. One of the quilts she worked on hangs in the Treasury House in Maryland. By 1981, she was the grand prize winner as designer in the Great Baltimore Best Quilting Contest. She has shown quilts nationally, won many awards, kept close to her quilting friends, and teaches quilting to senior citizens.

JEAN STANCLIFT, Lawrence, Kansas: Wreath of Strawberry Leaves.

Jean writes, "I began quilting in 1984 and have been addicted ever since. I belong to three quilt guilds and am Newsletter Editor for the Kaw Valley Quilt Guild. As the mother of two small children, I enjoy making wall and crib-size quilts."

JOANNE TURNLEY, Boulder, Colorado: Brenda's Rosebud Wreath, and Hospitality.

Joanne describes herself as a fairly new quilter with a background love of needlepoint and cross-stitch. She was originally a home economics teacher and now concentrates on hand quilting and piecing. Her beautiful Lesson Blocks attest to her versatility in appliqué as well.

GENE WAY, Davidsonville, Maryland: Love.

Gene has been sewing since she was seven. She began her first quilt, an heirloom "Turkey Tracks" in 1974, inspired by her husband's grandmother. Gene teaches senior citizens and concentrates her interests on clothing and smaller projects. Her hint: "Warm-up on an 'exercise' block for a few minutes before you start to quilt or appliqué, just like any exercise."

CAROL JO WHITE, Dunnellon, Florida: Co-quilting of quilt #6, "The Good Ladies of Baltimore."

Carol appreciates her exceptional quilting talent as God-given and the religious symbolism in the Baltimore Albums appeals to her. Her quilts right now are a series of originals on Biblical themes, with an Album Quilt waiting. She is married, has three sons, and is employed with Florida Power Corporation. "I jog, motorcycle, and attend college part-time." And quilts exquisitely!

The inscription of quilt #8, "Friendship's Offering," reads: "Friendship's Offering. When this you see/ Remember We/ Tho many a mile the distance be. To your friends you have been so good/ That we love you/ Is understood. To Mary Sue Hannan, May 4, 1987. Happy 70th Birthday!"

This quilt was a cooperative gift from these friends from Washington, D.C., Maryland, Virginia, Maine, and Australia: Margie Adamson, Boots Bartell, Barbara Bockman, Sarah Car-

michael, Hazel Carter, Lucia Clark, Jo Diggs, Kay Drury, Connie Dunlap, Carol Elliott, Bette Faries, Margerite Fleming, Kate Fowle, Pat Gallagher, Alice Geiger, Doris Gilbert, Peggy Goetz, Joy Graeub, Pat Hannan, Gwen Harris, Louise Hayes, Dianne Kernell, Ita Killeen, Kathryn Kuhn, Jackie Laudon, Kay Letteau, Carolyn Lynch, Frances Lynch, Kathy Mannix, Betty Martin, Barbara McConnell, Marjorie Mills, Toni Moore, Sheila Musselman, Ariella Niv, Betty Nock, Liz O'Brien, Bonnie Oliver, Lenore Parnham, Jane Phillips, Lynn Piper, Phyllis Pizzarro, Lee Porter, Donna Radner, Judy Rogers, Judy Seaver, Janet Sheridan, Elly Sienkiewicz, Ruth Stonely, Ellen Swanson, Nancy Tuckhorn, Kay Walker, Ruth Wiggins, Gayle Wistar, and Jean Wittig.

The quilt was quilted through Georgina Fries, by Emma and Fannie Hershberger. These two Amish sisters from Ohio sent this word, mid-way through: "We are quilting at it and aren't 1/2 done yet. It takes a lot of time. We thought it might go a month yet till we get it done, or maybe beginning of February. Just don't know yet. The butchering is now more over with so hope we can be more at quilting."

Part Four: The Patterns

These patterns are given on one, two, and four pages. The pattern transfer method depends on the number of pages and is explained in "Part One: Getting Started." Patterns are presented on the outside corner of each page for easy tracing. When I have had to make up a name for a pattern, I note this with an asterisk(*). Symbolic meanings given for the appliqué motifs were taken from *Spoken Without a Word*.

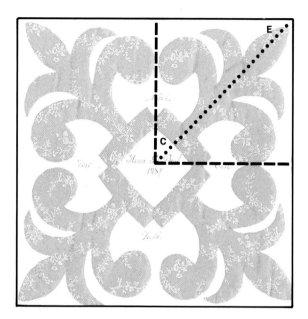

PATTERN #1: "Fleur-de-Lis I"

Lesson 1

Type: Classic "Baltimore"

The fleur-de-lis represents "The flame of Light, Life, and Power," the Trinity, and "Heaven's Queen." It is also the national emblem of France. It is seen repeatedly in the classic quilts in innumerable creative versions.

   Typically made in Turkey red (occasionally Victoria green), this design (and any large, simple, one-color pattern) looks good in a medium-to-large print.

PATTERN #2: "Double Hearts"

Lesson 1

Type: Classic "Baltimore"

Hearts abound in the classic quilts. They seem always to be in Turkey red. Versions of this strongly German-influenced *scherenschnitte* ("paper-cuttings") block occur with some frequency. This one is from a circa 1847-50 quilt in the Baltimore Museum of Art (catalog #15).

The original block may have been cut "freehand" from folded fabric. It is less defined than the pattern I have drafted. The original looks more like a puffed-up sugar cookie. You can make this simple shape quite elegant by using a striking large print or follow the classic original with solid red.

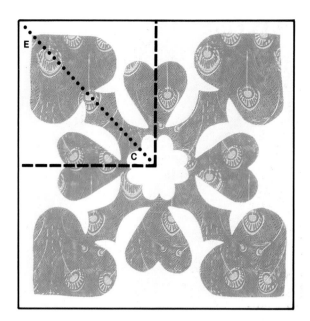

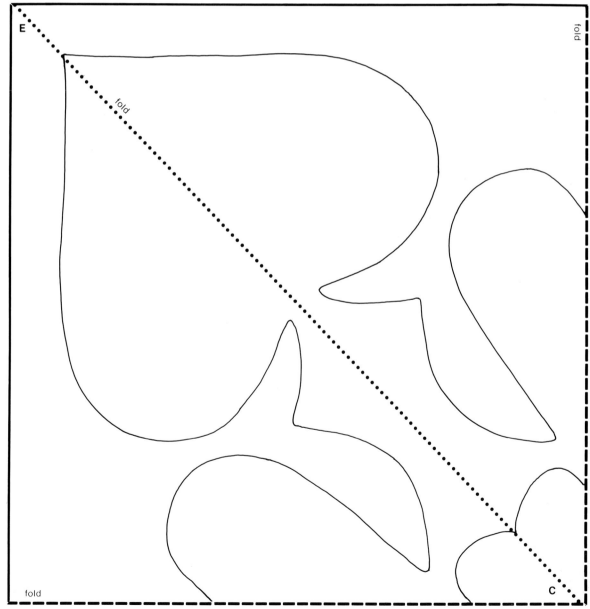

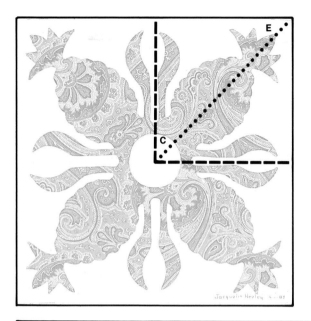

PATTERN #3: "You Are Perfect"*

Lesson 2

Type: Classic period, but "Beyond"

From Chambersberg, Pennsylvania, this is dated 1852.

Patterns cut from one piece of cloth occurred frequently in classic Maryland quilts from Baltimore County and nearby areas, including the heavily German Carroll and Frederick counties, and adjacent Pennsylvania. *Scherenschnitte* ("paper-cuttings") most probably influenced these designs.

Pineapples, meaning "You are perfect" and hospitality were a popular motif in the classic quilts. Most "Baltimore" versions are in the layered appliqué more frequently used in the Baltimore-style quilts.

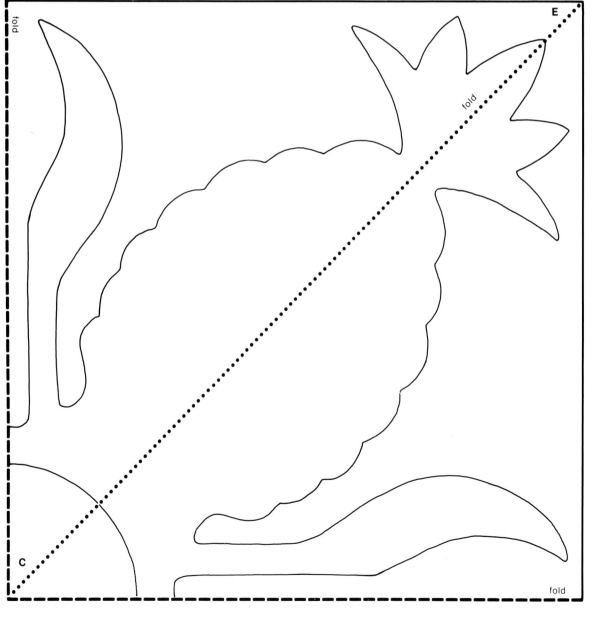

PATTERN #4: "Divine Guidance I (and II)"*

Lesson 4

Type: "Beyond"

My variation of a Baltimore block, this is from the same quilt as Pattern #2.

Stars in general symbolize divine guidance. Several multipointed stars together stand for Heaven. There are references in classic Album Quilts to heroes of the Mexican-American War. Thus a Lone Star might sometimes symbolize Texas. Stars of all sorts were exceedingly popular in the classic Albums. "Divine Guidance II" is "Baltimore" except that in the original, the small eight-pointed stars are solid.

In "Divine Guidance II" only, add the six green points as separate motifs to be layered under the red star. In the original, these points are green. Transfer this pattern by fourths, not eighths.

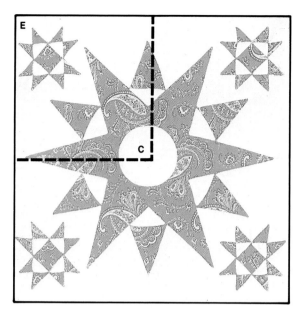

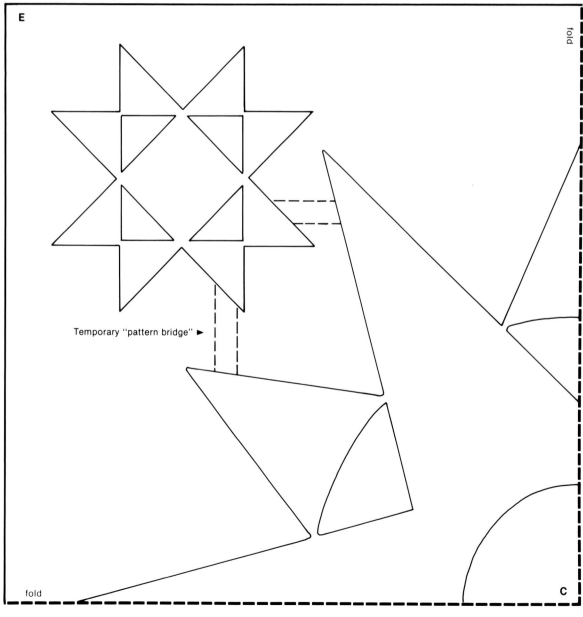

Temporary "pattern bridge" ▶

fold

E

fold

C

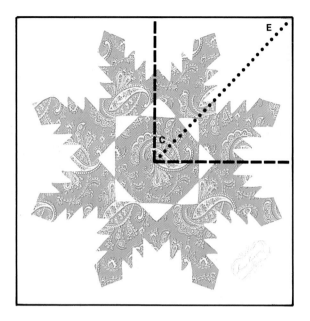

PATTERN #5: "Feathered Star"

Lesson 4

Type: Baltimore-style

From "Sarah McIlwain's Quilt," circa 1850+ (*Quilter's Newsletter Magazine*, #202).

Proof-positive that this was the heydey of appliqué! I think virtually no quiltmaker in the 1970s would have made this pattern by any method but piecing. Our sisters of long ago took on the challenge of executing it in appliqué. The delightful truth of the matter is, it is so much easier this way! If you are as careful about points and corners as Donna Carman was in making the model, your results will be exquisite.

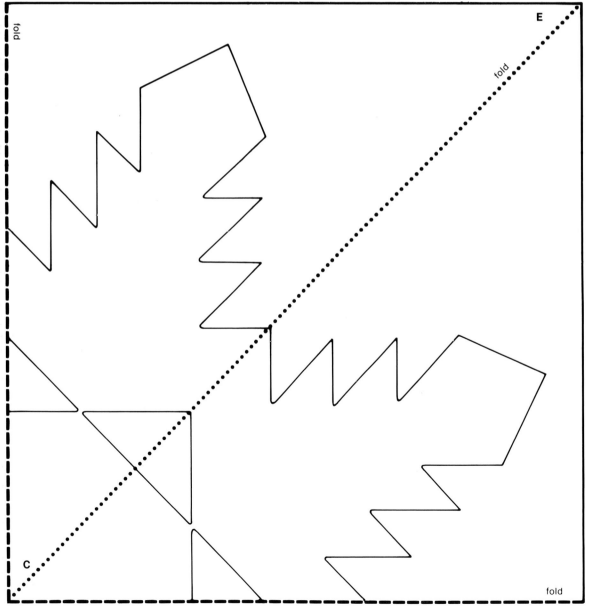

PATTERN #6: "Star of Hearts"*

Lesson 4

Type: "Beyond" Baltimore

From "The Mrs. Waterbury Album Quilt...New Jersey...1853" (*Quilts and Coverlets from the American Museum in Britain*, p. 85).

Hearts were a popular *paper-cut* motif. To Victorians, hearts meant, variously, charity, piety, devotion, and, of course, love. With stars meaning divine guidance, this block could mean devotion to God, Heaven-sent love, or could express a wish that the love would be Heaven blessed. This is a charming, relatively quick block.

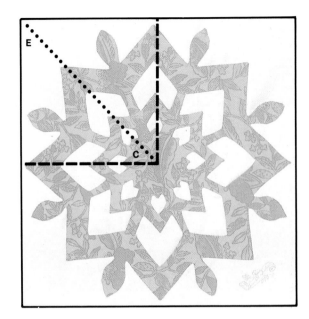

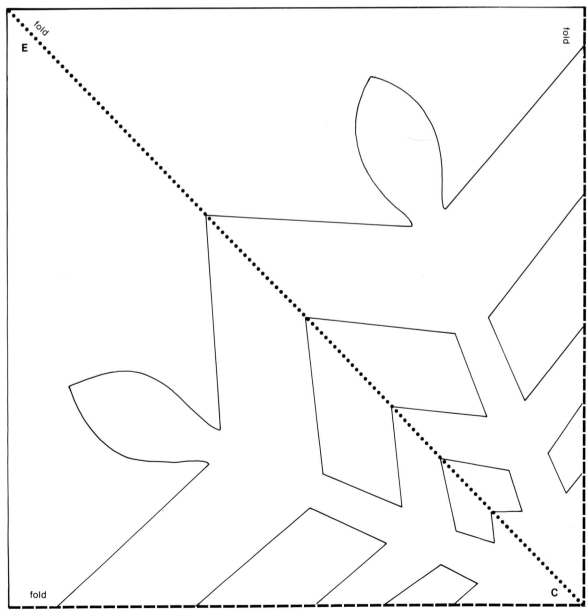

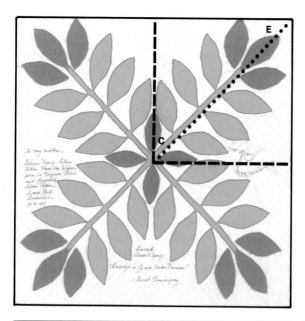

PATTERN #7: "Crossed Laurel Sprays"*

Lesson 5

Type: "Baltimore"

Versions of this block appear frequently in the classic quilts.

A crown of laurel has symbolized triumph, victory, success, and renown since antiquity. The laurel can also mean pride and good fortune.

By symbolic intent alone, the laurel merits inclusion in a Presentation Album Quilt. (Many of us would count ourselves successful indeed, simply to receive a Presentation Quilt.) Perhaps it was popular also because it could be made by unit cutwork, an easy way to approach the tedium of stems and leaves.

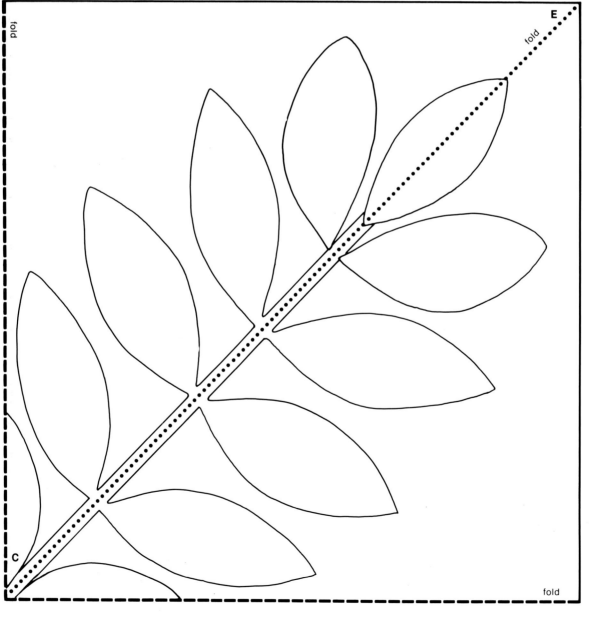

PATTERN #8: "$200,000 Tulips"*

Lesson 5

Type: Classic "Baltimore"

Circa 1840.

This is a facetious name for the oft-presented red tulip which means "A declaration of love!" This is one of two versions in quilt #2 which last sold in January 1987 for "at least $200,000," according to the dealer. Monetary value aside, tulips bloom profusely in classic Baltimore Album Quilts and you will find planting this one in yours a happy experience.

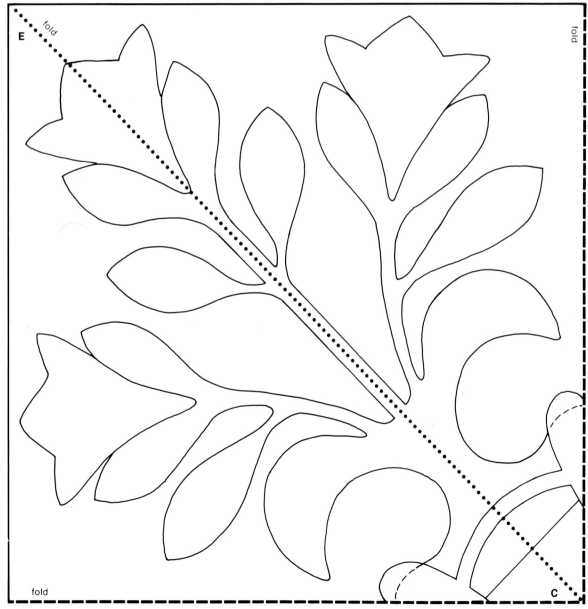

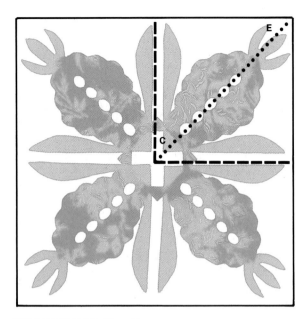

PATTERN #9: "Hospitality"*

Lesson 5

Type: Baltimore-style

From the Major Ringgold Quilt, circa 1846, Shelburne Museum, Shelburne, Vermont.

This is a wonderfully graphic pattern in Turkey red and apple green in the original (pictured in *An American Sampler*). Were you to compare your finished block to the classic one, I think you would be pleased at how precise the design has become through your use of pattern bridges and freezer paper on the top.

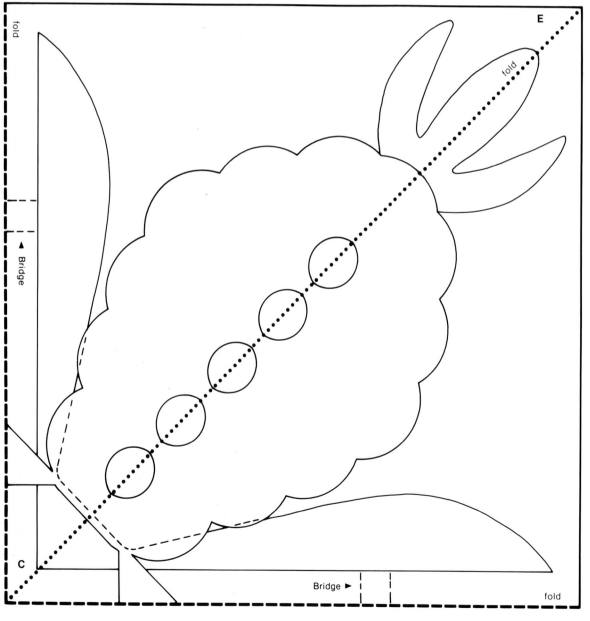

PATTERN #10: "Fleur-de-Lis with Folded Rosebuds II"*

Lesson 6

Type: "Beyond"

This is "Beyond" in my addition of the folded roses, but otherwise it's a faithful replica of the one found in the circa 1852 Baltimore Album Quilt made for Miss Isabella Battee, now in the Baltimore Museum of Art.

This is one of the most often repeated designs in the classic quilts. It is both lovely in appearance and in thought. It is symbolic, with the fleur-de-lis (see Pattern #1) and the rose which stands for love. The square of the wreath symbolizes earthly matters, as circular wreaths symbolize heavenly or eternal matters.

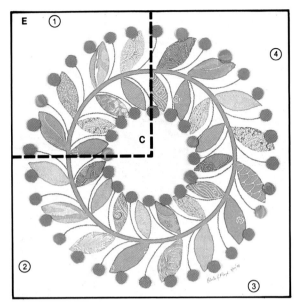

PATTERN #11: "Wreath of Cherries"*

Lesson 9

Type: Baltimore-style

This block is the important center block, from the same quilt as Pattern #9.

These additional instructions are useful: The circle wreath is most easily accomplished by sewing the inside seam on the sewing machine. To complete the full-wreath circle, tuck one end of your stem strip inside the other, plug and socket fashion. These are smaller stuffed cherries. Use a quarter as a template, but this time, sew the running stitches 1/8" inside the drawn circle.

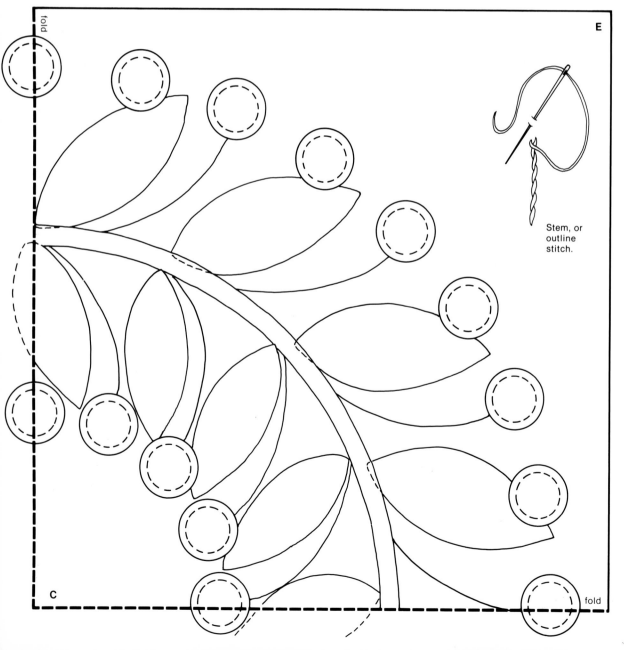

Stem, or outline stitch.

PATTERN #12: "Brenda's Rosebud Wreath"*

Lesson 6

Type: "Beyond"

This is an original design by Brenda Papadakis. She adapted the center from an 1825 Ohio Rose pattern. (My folded roses are an optional addition.)

If one were to read a symbolic message into this block, it would be "eternal love," the circular wreath meaning eternal (or heavenly), and the roses meaning love. In Brenda's original, each wedge of the center is a separately appliquéd motif in shades of red and rose. Done this way, the block could be read as a "Crown of Roses," which means "superior merit." Transfer this pattern by tracing it counterclockwise on each quadrant of your folded paper.

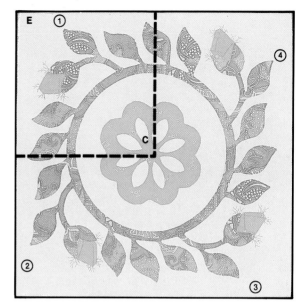

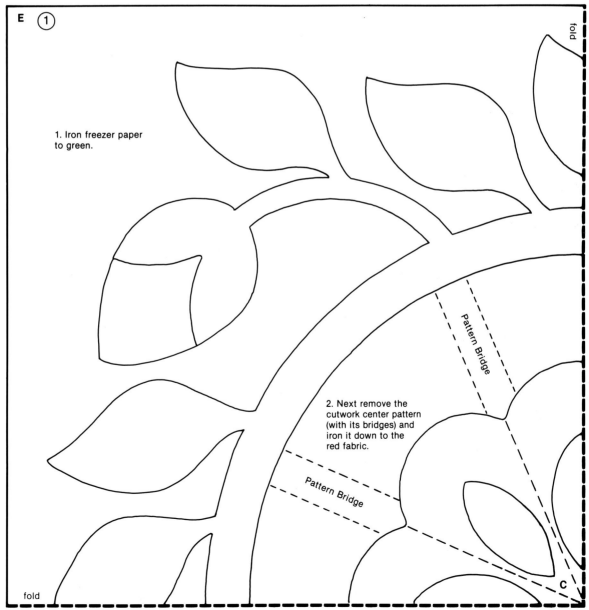

E ①

1. Iron freezer paper to green.

Pattern Bridge

2. Next remove the cutwork center pattern (with its bridges) and iron it down to the red fabric.

Pattern Bridge

fold

C

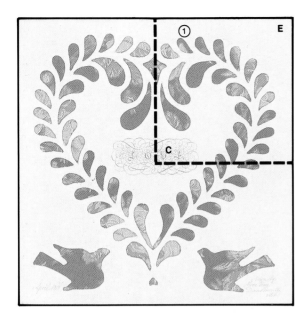

PATTERN #13: "Love"* or "Feather-Wreathed Heart with Doves"*

Lesson 3

Type: "Beyond"

This is my original design. Feather-weathed circles are the classic version. The doves are from classic Victorian blocks.

Hearts mean love, charity, piety, or devotion, while doves symbolize purity, peace, innocence, or the Holy Spirit. There are meanings aplenty for including this block in any Presentation Quilt. In fact, I designed it because a feathered heart is irresistible and gives one good practice in inlaid appliqué.

PATTERN #13: "Love"* or "Feather-Wreathed Heart with Doves"*

Second page

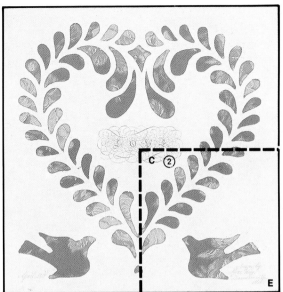

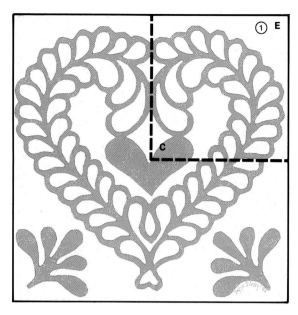

PATTERN #14: "Feather-Wreathed Heart"*

Lesson 3

Type: "Beyond"

Again, this is my original design, in classic style.

This is the same heart as Pattern #13, but now with an inner row of "petals." The outside of this design is done by onlaid cutwork appliqué. Then the petals are done by inlaid appliqué. Elegantly Victorian, this block by itself would make a nice commemorative certificate, framed to record a birth or marriage.

PATTERN #14: "Feather-Wreathed Heart"*

Second page

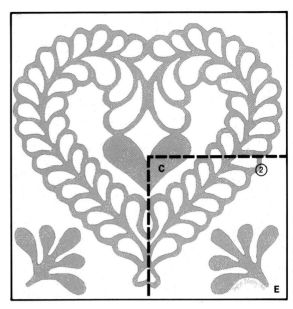

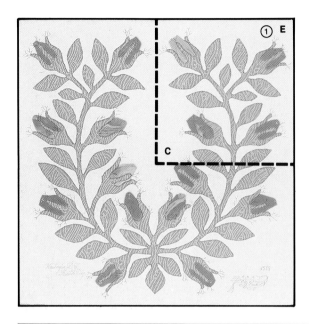

PATTERN #15: "Sweetheart Rose Lyre"*

Lesson 6

Type: "Baltimore" if made with flat roses, "Beyond" if made with folded circle roses

The original block is in the same quilt as Pattern #10.

Lyres appear over and over again in these classic quilts, both as the motif itself, or as floral wreaths. Lyres, or "David's Harp," symbolize "All music in honor of God." As an instrument of divine music, eternal music, they could intend "in memoriam" as well. Victorians were openly and demonstrably religious. Roses mean love. Thus the message here might be religious devotion or eternal love.

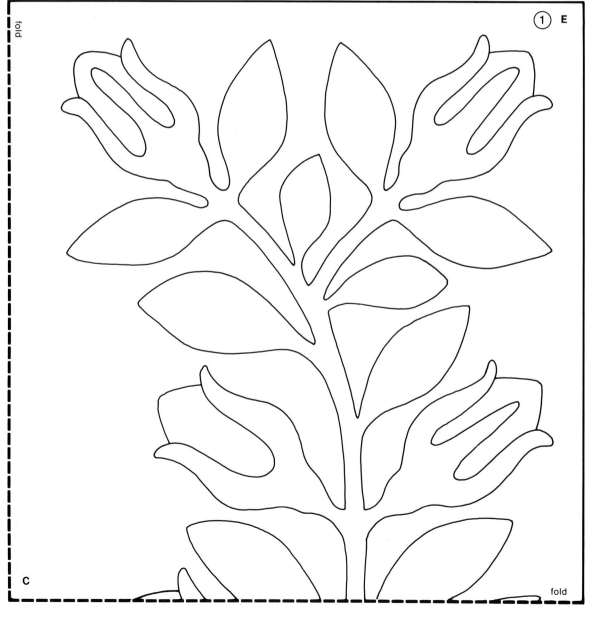

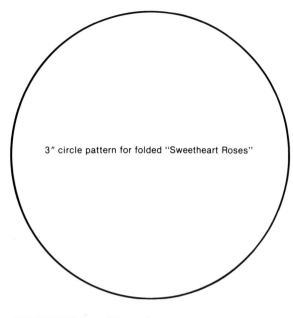

3″ circle pattern for folded "Sweetheart Roses"

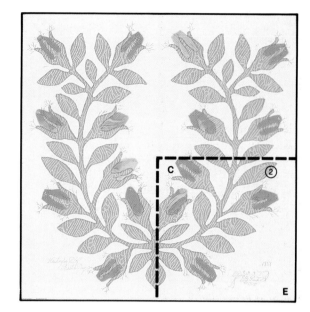

PATTERN #15: "Sweetheart Rose Lyre"*
Second page

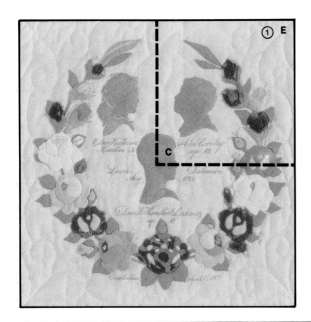

PATTERN #16: "Silhouette Wreath"*

Lesson 7

Type: "Beyond"

This is my adaptation (with folded rosebuds) of "Steamship Captain Russell" from the 1852 Baltimore Album in the Baltimore Museum of Art (catalog #23).

This block (shown on this book's front cover and as block A-2 in quilt #7) is a bit more complex than Pattern #15. Notice that in the upper-right third of the wreath, the stem itself has been interrupted by a tiny bud's stem which has to be slipped under it. Leave a space open waiting for it. I traced the silhouette portraits of our three children onto the block in permanent ink.

PATTERN #16: "Silhouette Wreath"*

Second page

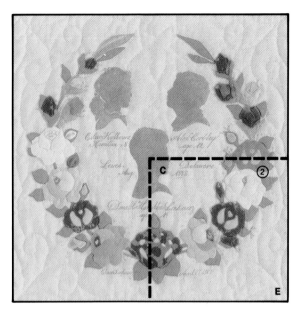

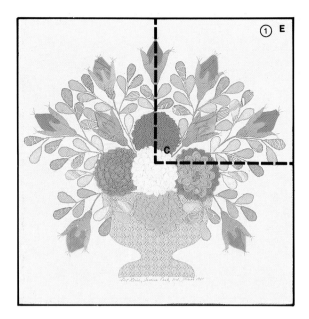

PATTERN #17: "A Token of Gratitude"*

Lesson 8

Type: Classic "Baltimore"-style

From the same quilt as Pattern #9.

In the language of flowers, a bouquet of full-blown roses is "A token of gratitude." Other possible intents to attach to this block are: "Love's Ambassador" (cabbage rose), "I love you" (full-blown rose), or "I am worthy of you" and "purity" (white rose). This block is a real challenge. Dot Reise notes that the embroidered stems should go on first, then the calyxes, then the rosebuds. Cleverly, she coiled the center of the white rose tighter, since it has to go over two already ruched roses.

For Stems: Stem or outline stitch.

PATTERN #17: "A Token of Gratitude"*

Second page

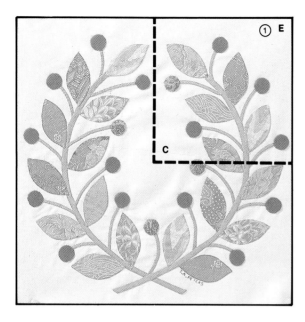

PATTERN #18: "Crown of Laurel/Broken Wreath of Cherries"*

Lesson 9

Type: "Beyond"

This is my adaptation of two blocks in a classic Baltimore Album, circa 1847-50 (Baltimore Museum of Art, catalog #16). This one is simpler, having fewer leaves and cherries.

The "Laurel and the Cherry" patterns are sometimes ambiguously similar. Thus my caution in naming this charming pattern. The "broken wreath" is how a "crown" was often depicted. If forced to choose, I would guess this is a Crown of Laurel, since the cherry is more likely to be depicted in a completed wreath.

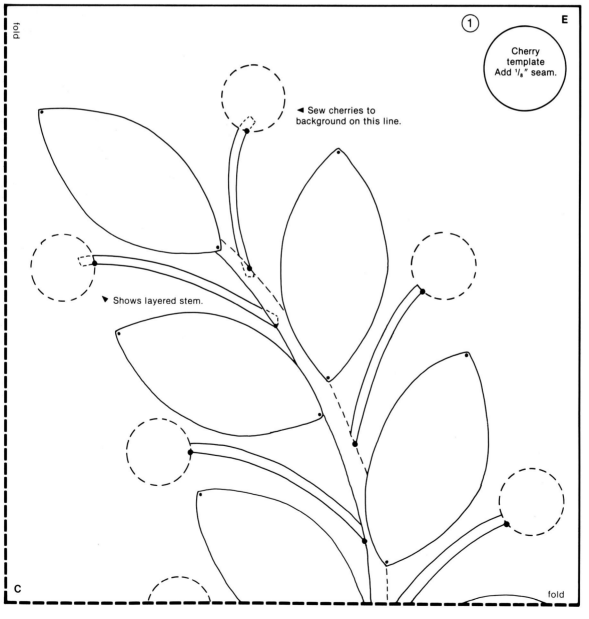

◄ Sew cherries to background on this line.

Cherry template
Add 1/8" seam.

▼ Shows layered stem.

PATTERN #18: "Crown of Laurel/Broken Wreath of Cherries"*

Second page

The congratulatory symbolism of laurel is detailed in Pattern #7. Cherries have homier meanings, but ones closer to the heart which is probably why they were a bit more popular.

Cherries mean sweet character or good deeds. Cherry twins mean love's charms and are a good luck symbol. Botanically, both are taken liberties with, for both cherry and laurel berries grow in clusters. But, by any measure, this berry wreath is a fruitful place for us to begin our "stuffed cherries."

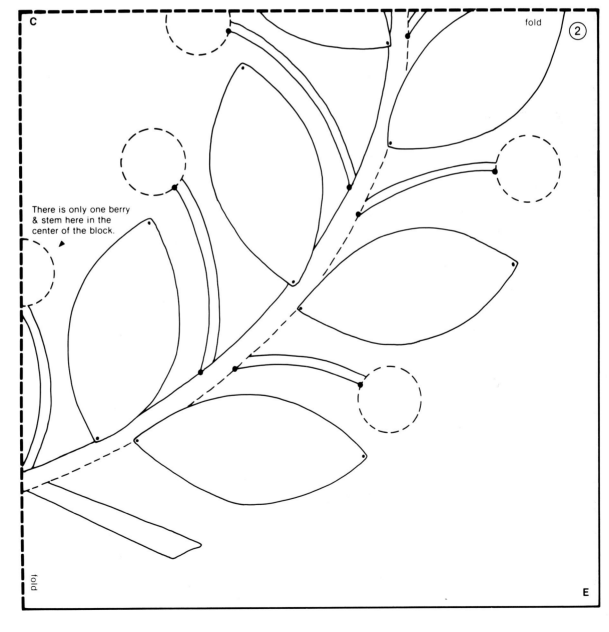

There is only one berry & stem here in the center of the block.

fold

C

fold

E

②

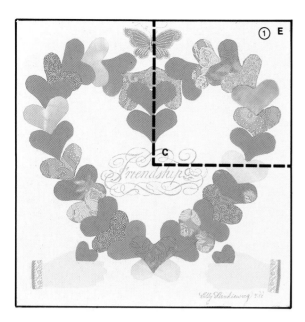

PATTERN #19: "Wreath of Hearts I (and II)"*

Lesson 10

Type: Classic "Baltimore"

Circa 1850, pictured in *The Quilt Engagement Calendar Treasury* (p. 148).

The model is my adaptation of this classic pattern. Another version within the same classic quilt is a circular wreath of hearts, simple enough to make even without a pattern. The two make a balancing pair, one on either side of a row of blocks.

The block pictured here (Version II) uses a wide variety of beautiful fabrics. If this is not to your taste, you'll appreciate knowing that the original block is made all of one green calico (green with a small black print) and solid Turkey red.

PATTERN #19: "Wreath of Hearts I (and II)"*

Second page

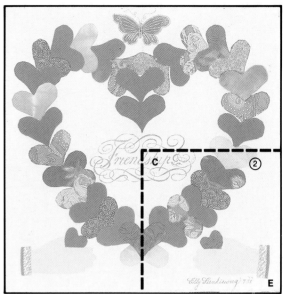

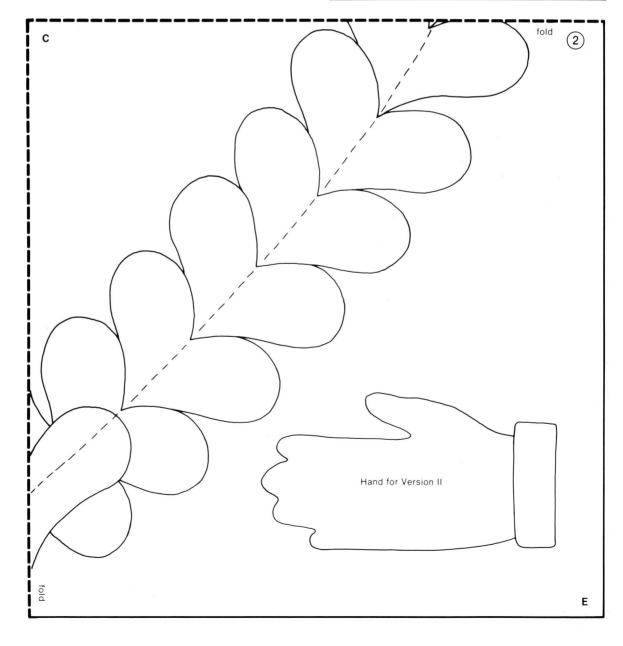

Hand for Version II

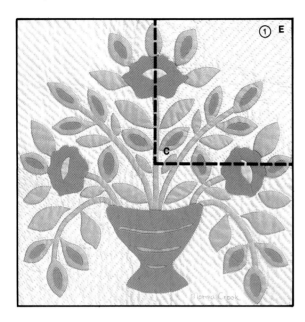

PATTERN #20: "Vase of Roses I"*

Lesson 10

Type: Classic "Baltimore"

From the same quilt as Pattern #19.

Full of amatory meaning, this charming vase of roses could well be done in seams-basted-under appliqué. It involves just three colors, but offers layered flowers, superfine stems, lots of leaves, and an inlaid vase. The model was masterfully made by Nonna Crook who used freezer paper ironed to the wrong side of the appliqués, then simply needleturned against the crisp edge it provided.

PATTERN #20: "Vase of Roses I"*

Second page

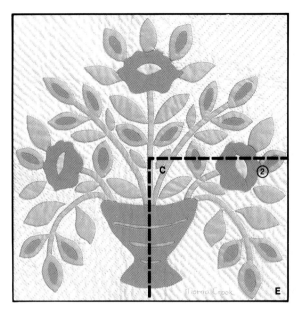

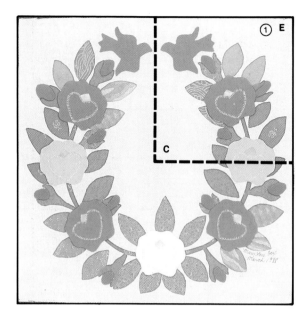

PATTERN # 21: "Rose Wreath with Red Birds"*

Lesson 11

Type: Classic "Baltimore"

From a Baltimore Quilt, dated 1854, in Winterthur Museum.

Mary Lou Fox, who made our model, included these notes: "Used freezer paper on top except on hearts to be buttonholed. It went slowly, took 30 hours, enjoyed it."

This is a lovely block on which to try hemmed-edge buttonholing. It is very Victorian-looking but not overly ornate. The colors in our model are those of the original.

PATTERN #21: "Rose Wreath with Red Birds"*

Second page

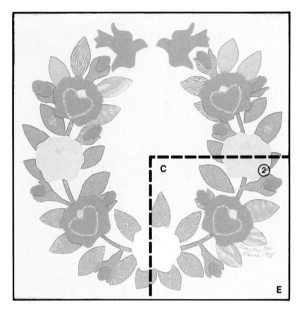

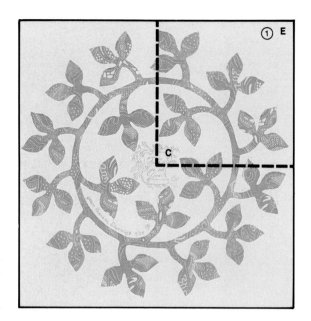

PATTERN #22: "Wreath of Strawberry Leaves"*

Lesson 2

Type: Classic "Baltimore"

This block is from a quilt captioned "d.1846, Baltimore, Maryland."

This block is from a quilt which is rare in its diagonal set. (Most Baltimore Albums are set square.) It appears in Kolter's *Forget Me Not* (p. 29).

Strawberry leaves mean completion and perfection. They are usually depicted with the strawberry itself, which symbolizes esteem and love, intoxication and delight. Among the many other symbols in this quilt are tulips ("A declaration of love!" in the language of the flowers), and a dog, meaning fidelity. These symbols strongly suggest a Bride's Quilt.

PATTERN #22: "Wreath of Strawberry Leaves"*

Second page

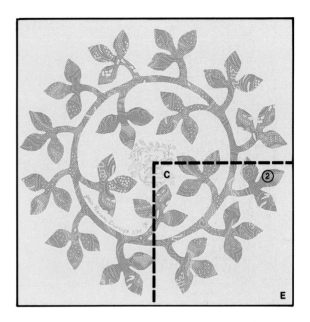

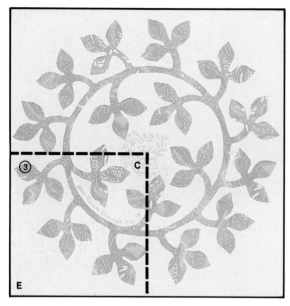

PATTERN #22: "Wreath of Strawberry Leaves"*

Third page

PATTERN #22: "Wreath of Strawberry Leaves"*

Fourth page

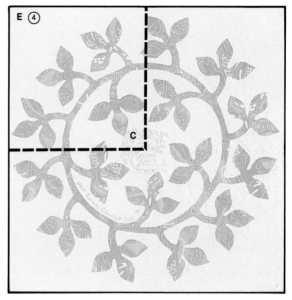

PATTERN #23: "Lyre Wreath"*

Lesson 7

Type: "Beyond"

The original Lyre is from a block of the Washington Monument in Baltimore (see Photo 5). The "marriage" center is my design. Joy Nichols, however, made her own original version, dressing the loving couple in period costume. The bride's lace veil which lets her dress show through is particularly charming.

"Divine music" and "love" are the intertwined symbols here. Perhaps the literal message of such a block would be "blissful harmony" or "blessed by God." Other possibilities for this block's center would be an angel in it, or a verse or inscription done in beautiful calligraphy. ("Marriage" here was originally done by George Bickham in the eighteenth century.)

◄ Stuffed Rose

fold

PATTERN #23: "Lyre Wreath"*

Second page

Layered Rose ▶

PATTERN #23: "Lyre Wreath"*

Third page

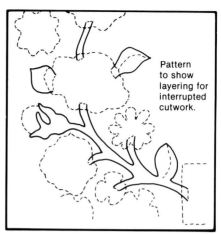

Pattern
to show
layering for
interrupted
cutwork.

Cutwork
Rose ▶

PATTERN #23: "Lyre Wreath"*

Fourth page

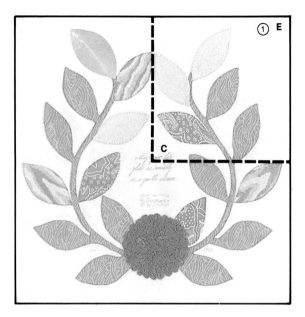

PATTERN #24: "Ruched Rose Lyre"*

Lesson 8

Type: "Beyond"

My version of a ruched rose lyre is from the same quilt as Pattern #22.

The original of this block had three red leaves (possibly buds?) atop each lyre stem, as with the Crossed Laurel Sprays (Pattern #7). I drew the one here from memory, leaving the red leaves out. This one also has fewer leaves than the original.

This block is a pure delight to make. If I had to make blocks for several Presentation Quilts, this would be the one I would do repeatedly. It is dramatic, interesting, and relatively fast.

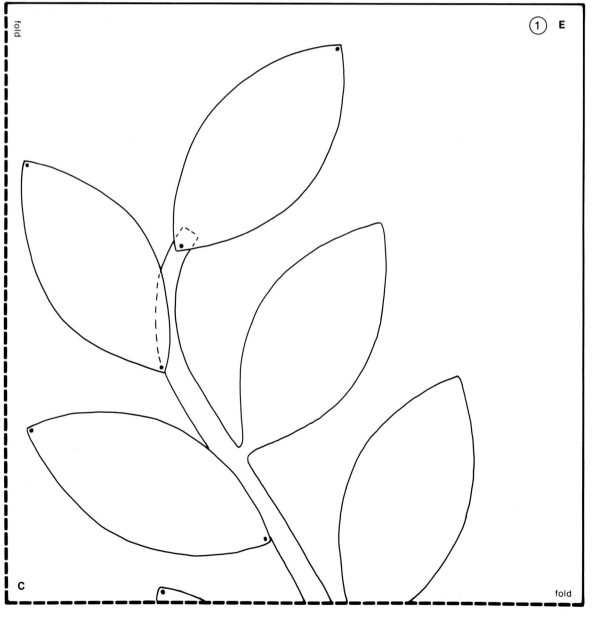

PATTERN #24: "Ruched Rose Lyre"*

Second page

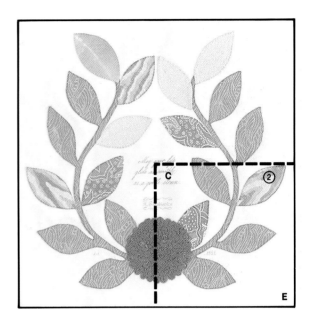

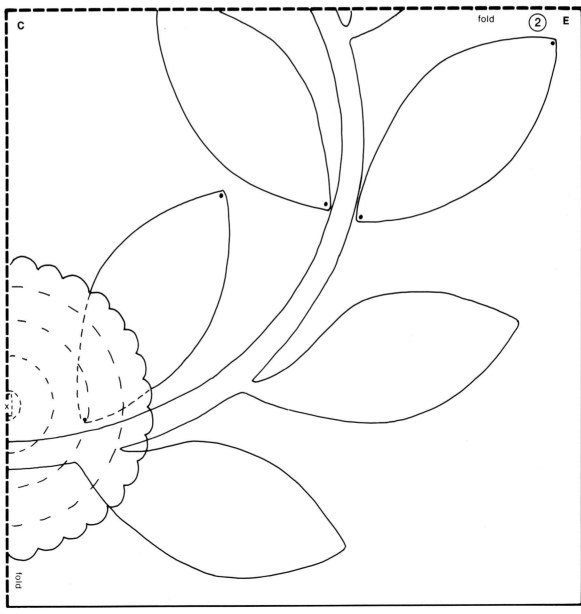

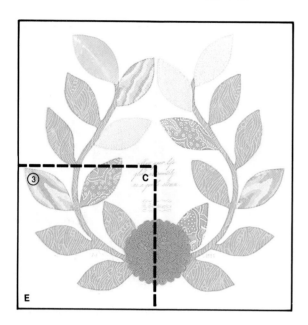

PATTERN #24: "Ruched Rose Lyre"*

Third page

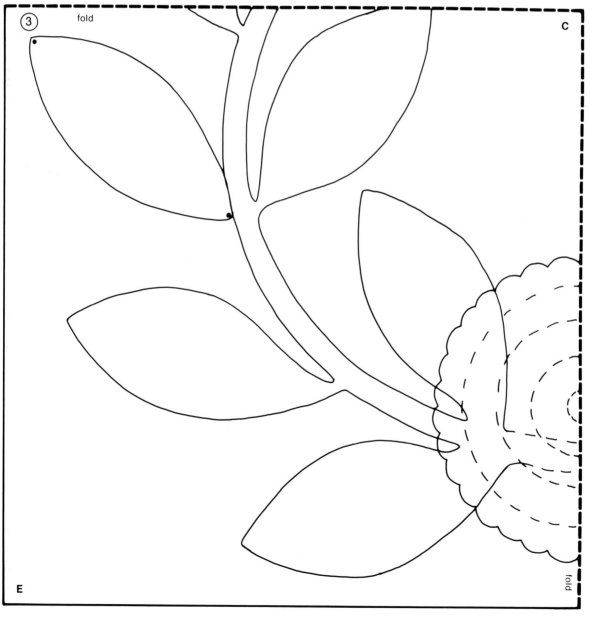

PATTERN #24: "Ruched Rose Lyre"*

Fourth page

When all the cutwork is appliquéd, mark the background fabric:

1. Mark a tiny dot to show where each separately added leaf goes.

2. Mark the dotted lines where your ruched strip goes. Mark an "X" where its sewing is begun.

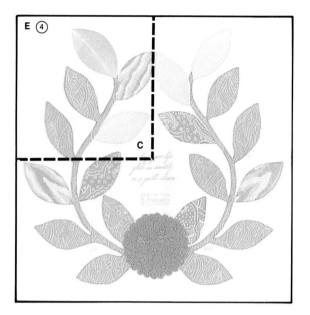

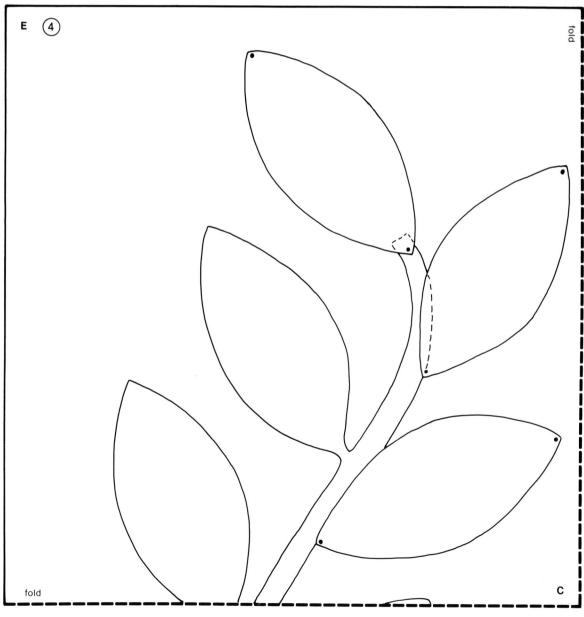

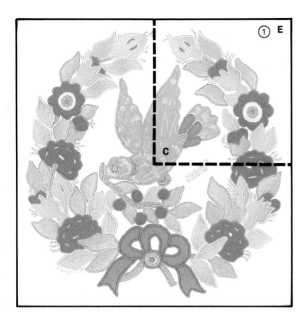

PATTERN #25: "Wreath and Dove"*

Lesson 11

Type: "Baltimore"

From Lee Porter's dated 1846-47 quilt, quilt #4.

Templates for the "Wreath and Dove" pattern are drawn with the assumption that you will add 1/4" all around each one, then cut it back to the 1/32" raw edge allowance as you sew. Detailed directions for this are in Lesson 11.

The classic fabrics of this block's original are shaded or plain solids, except for the typically representational use of prints for textures on the bird, its bright eye, and the centers of the full-blown flowers.

PATTERN #25: "Wreath and Dove"*

Second page

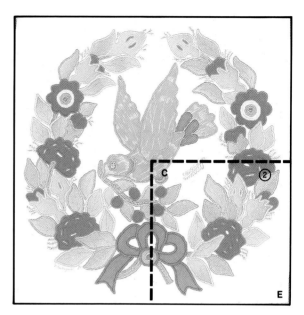

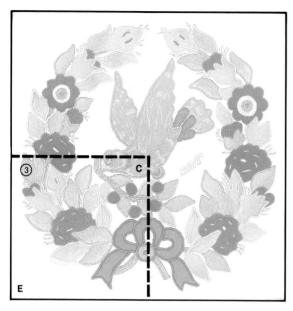

PATTERN #25: "Wreath and Dove"*

Third page

The pale circle is inlaid, not buttonholed.

PATTERN #25: "Wreath and Dove"*

Fourth page

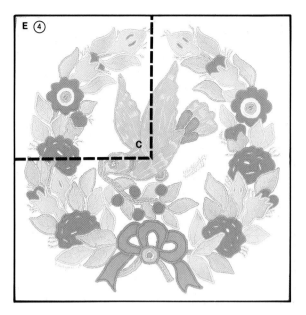

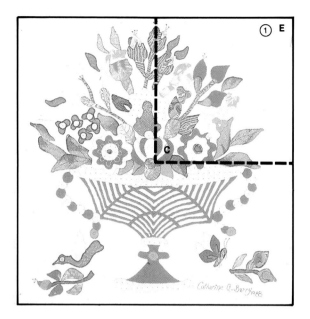

PATTERN #26: "Red Woven Basket of Flowers"*

Lesson 12

Type: Classic "Baltimore"-style

From a circa 1850 Album Quilt in the Abby Aldrich Rockefeller Museum.

The more realistic Victorian patterns joyfully pictured the interior decor accoutrements of the day. Woven red baskets were clearly the height of fashion for they were often depicted, particularly in the quilt block style attributed in *Baltimore Album Quilts* to Mary Evans. This pattern is clearly a challenge to make, but Cathy Berry has replicated the graceful original to perfection.

This quilt is pictured in Kolter's *Forget Me Not* (frontispiece) and in *America's Quilts and Coverlets* (pp. 148-49).

PATTERN #26: "Red Woven Basket of Flowers"*

Second page

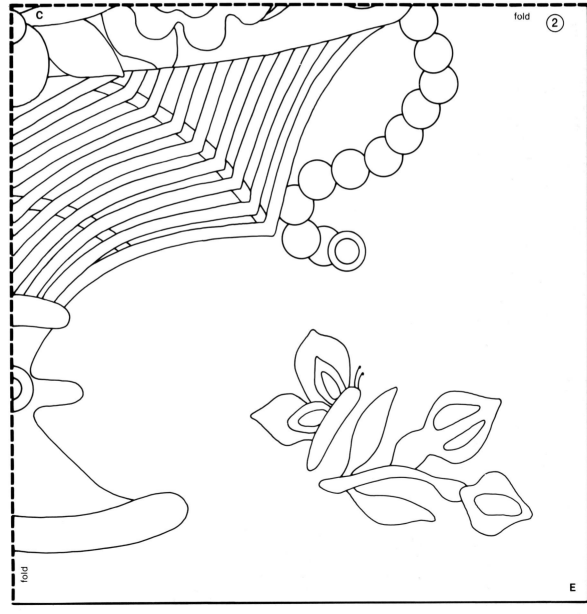

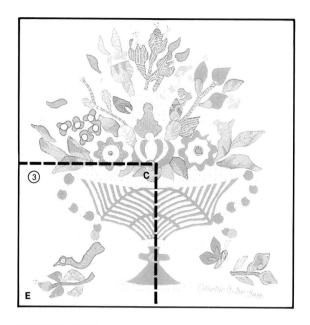

PATTERN #26: "Red Woven Basket of Flowers"*

Third page

PATTERN #26: "Red Woven Basket of Flowers"*

Fourth page

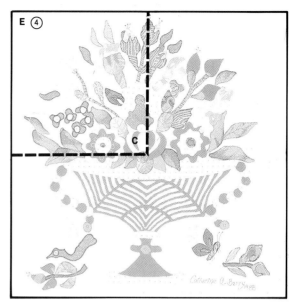

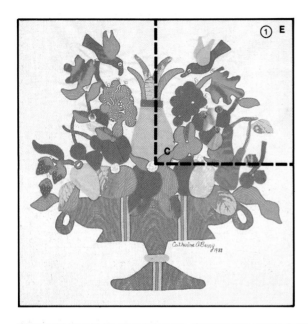

PATTERN #27: "Epergne of Fruit"*

Lesson 12

Type: Classic "Baltimore"

Epergnes, raised compote centerpieces for holding fruit or desserts, had recently become the style when the classic Baltimore Album Quilts were made. They proudly reflect many versions but are often in blue cut-glass. This one is in the shape of a classic Greek kylix or drinking cup, reflecting the Victorian's fondness for the Greek Revival Style. Much monumental architecture in the Nation's Capital also embodies this nineteenth-century revival in marble.

PATTERN #27: "Epergne of Fruit"*

Second page

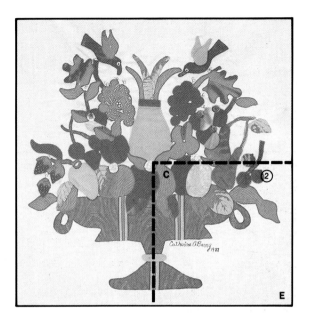

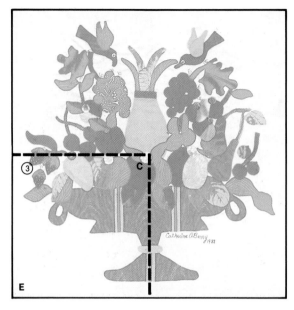

PATTERN #27: "Epergne of Fruit"*

Third page

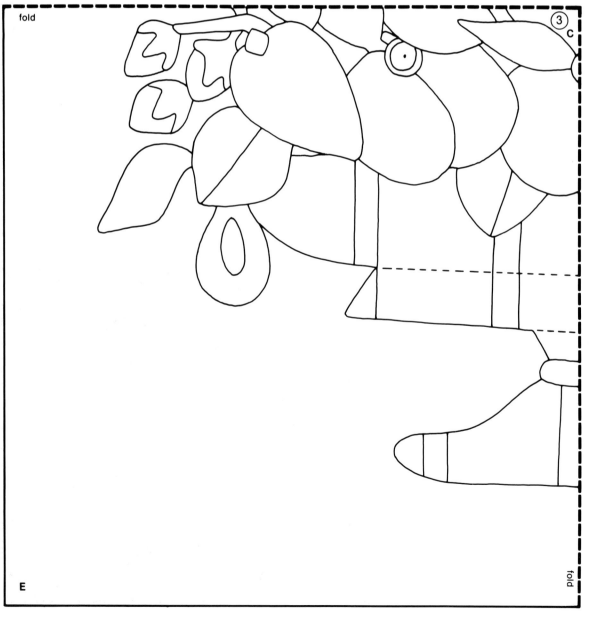

PATTERN #27: "Epergne of Fruit"*

Fourth page

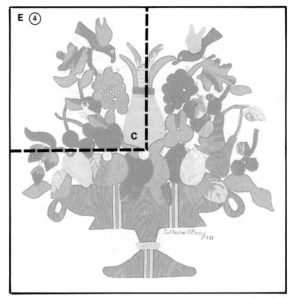

Bibliography

HISTORY AND DESIGN BACKGROUND

Barber, Lynn. *The Heyday of Natural History*. Doubleday, New York, 1980.
Beirne, Francis. *The Amiable Baltimoreans*. Johns Hopkins University Press, Baltimore, Md., 1984.
Bickham, George. *The Universal Penman*. (Originally published by George Bickham, London, circa 1740-41.) Dover, New York, 1954.
Bordes, Marilyn. *Twelve Great Quilts from the American Wing*. Metropolitan Museum of Art, New York, 1974.
Colby, Averil. *Patchwork*. B. T. Botsford, Ltd., London, 1973.
Cunz, D. *The Maryland Germans, A History*. Princeton University Press, Princeton, N.J., 1948.
Dunton, William Rush, Jr. *Old Quilts*. Published by the author, Catonsville, Md., 1946.
Jones, Owen. *The Grammar of Ornament: All 100 Color Plates from the Folio Edition of the Great Victorian Scrapbook of Historic Design*. (First published in England, 1856.) Portland House, New York, 1986.
Katzenberg, Dena. *Baltimore Album Quilts*. Baltimore Museum of Art, Baltimore, Md., 1981.
Nelson, Cyril, editor. *The Quilt Engagement Calendar*. Dutton, New York, 1983, 1984, 1985, 1987, 1988.
Orlofsky, Patsy and Myron. *Quilts in America*. McGraw-Hill, New York, 1974.
Rae, Janet. *The Quilts of the British Isles*. Dutton, New York, 1987.
Sienkiewicz, Elly. "My Baltimore Album Quilt Discoveries." *Quilter's Newsletter Magazine*, #202, May 1988, pp. 26-27.
_____. *Spoken Without a Word: A Lexicon of Selected Symbols with 24 Patterns from Classic Baltimore Album Quilts*. Published by the author, Washington, D.C., 1983.
Wright, Roxa. "Baltimore Friendship Quilt," *Woman's Day*, October 1965.

SYMBOLISM, AND SYMBOLISM IN THE CLASSIC ALBUM QUILTS

Cirlot, Juan Eduardo. *A Dictionary of Symbols*. Translated by Jack Sage. Philosophical Library, New York, 1962.
Ferguson, George. *Signs & Symbols in Christian Art*. Oxford University Press, New York, 1954.
Peroni, Laura. *The Language of Flowers*. Crown, New York, 1982.
Sienkiewicz, Elly. *Spoken Without a Word: A Lexicon of Selected Symbols with 24 Patterns from Classic Baltimore Album Quilts*. Published by the author, Washington, D.C., 1983.
Spencer, F. *Chrismons, An Explanation of the Symbols on the Chrismons Tree at the Ascension Lutheran Church in Danville, Virginia*. Womack Press, Danville, Va., 1970.

PICTURES OF APPLIQUÉ ALBUM QUILTS

Allen, Gloria Seaman. *Old Line Traditions, Maryland Women and Their Quilts*. DAR Museum, Washington, D.C.,1985.
Bacon, Lenice Ingram. *American Patchwork Quilts*. Morrow, New York, 1973.
Bank, Mirra, compiler. *Anonymous Was a Woman*. St. Martin's Press, New York, 1979.
Bath, Virginia. *Needlework in America: History, Designs, and Techniques*. Viking Press, New York, 1979.
Betterton, Shiela. *Quilts and Coverlets from the American Museum in Britain*. Butler & Tanner, London, 1978, 1982.
Bishop, Robert. *The Knopf Collectors' Guides to American Antiques*. Knopf, New York, 1982.
_____. *New Discoveries in American Quilts*. Dutton, New York, 1975.
Bullard, Lacy Folmar, and Shiell, Betty Jo. *Chintz Quilts: Unfading Glory*. Serendipity Publishers, Tallahassee, Fla., 1983.
Fox, Sandi. *Small Endearments: Nineteenth-century Quilts for Children*. Scribner, New York, 1985.
Hinson, Dolores. *American Graphic Quilt Designs*. Arco, New York, 1983.
Houck, Carter, and Nelson, Cyril. *The Quilt Engagement Calendar Treasury*. Dutton, New York, 1982.
Katzenberg, Dena. *Baltimore Album Quilts*. Baltimore Museum of Art, Baltimore, Md., 1981.
Kolter, Jane Bentley. *Forget Me Not: A Gallery of Friendship and Album Quilts*. Main Street Press, Pittstown, N.J., 1985.
Lasansky, Jeannette. *In the Heart of Pennsylvania*. Oral Traditions Project of the Union County Historical Society, Lewisburg, Pa., 1985.

_____. *In the Heart of Pennsylvania, Symposium Papers*. Oral Traditions Project of the Union County Historical Society, Lewisburg, Pa., 1986.

_____. *Pieced by Mother: Over One Hundred Years of Quiltmaking Traditions*. The Oral Traditions Project of the Union County Historical Society, Lewisburg, Pa., 1987.

Lipman, Jean, and Winchester, Alice. *The Flowering of American Folk Art, 1776-1876*. Running Press, Philadelphia, Pa., 1974.

Orlofsky, Patsy and Myron. *Quilts in America*. McGraw-Hill, New York, 1974.

Quilt Digest. Numbers 1 and 2. Kiracofe and Kile, San Francisco, 1983, 1984.

Quilt Digest. Numbers 3, 4, and 5. Quilt Digest Press, San Francisco, 1987.

Safford, Carleton, and Bishop, Robert. *America's Quilts and Coverlets*. Weathervane Books/Dutton, New York, 1972.

Smyth, Frances P., and Yakush, Mary, editors. *An American Sampler: Folk Art from the Shelburne Museum*. National Gallery of Art, Washington, D.C., 1987.

Ungerleider-Mayerson, Joy. *Jewish Folk Art from Biblical Days to Modern Times*. Summit Books, New York, 1986.

Woodward, Thomas, and Greenstein, Blanche. *Crib Quilts and Other Small Wonders*. Dutton, New York, 1981.

BALTIMORE ALBUM QUILT PATTERNS AND APPLIQUÉ HOW-TO

Boyink, Betty. *Flower Gardens and Hexagons for Quilters*. Published by the author, Grand Haven, Mich., 1984.

Hinson, Dolores. *American Graphic Quilt Designs*. Arco, New York, 1983.

Patera, Charlotte. *Cutwork Appliqué*. New Century, Pittstown, N.J., 1983.

Sienkiewicz, Elly. *Spoken Without a Word: A Lexicon of Selected Symbols with 24 Patterns from Classic Baltimore Album Quilts*. Published by the author, Washington, D.C., 1983.

Appendix I: Sources

If, after checking with your local quilt shop, you are still looking for a special service or supply, this brief listing may help.

COMMISSIONED QUILTING AND BINDING

Bellwether Dry Goods, Georgina B. Fries, P.O. Box #6, Lothian, MD 20711, 301-867-0665. Complete quilting service, new or antique tops. Custom quilts made to order. Victorian American linens, antique fabrics, and related sewing items.

PATTERNS

Anna Holland, P.O. Box 161, Waterford, VA 22190. "Mini-Madness": Anna's original design miniature Baltimore Album Quilt, complete pattern, $5.75 postage paid.
Spoken Without a Word: A Lexicon of Selected Symbols with 24 Patterns from Classic Baltimore Album Quilts. $16.95 plus $3.00 handling. Elly Sienkiewicz, 5540 30th Street N.W., Washington, DC 20015.
Osage County Quilt Factory, 400 Walnut, Overbrook, KS 66524. "Kansas Album Quilt: Baltimore-style Album Quilt Pattern for 14" Blocks," $10.75 postage paid.

SPECIAL SUPPLIES

Bellwether Enterprises, R.D. 3, Box 416, Ringoes, NJ 08551. Complete line of laser-cut plastic templates, kits, patterns, and supplies for Template Appliqué™.
Cabin Fever Calicoes, P.O. Box 550106, Atlanta, GA 30355. Catalog, $2.00. Unique source of quilting supplies for Baltimore Album Quilts: opaque projector, lightboxes, background fabric, floral fabric color-paks, tie-dyed fabric, hand-painted silks for stuffed roses, permanent pens, *Copperplate Manual*, freezer paper for overseas quilters, etc.
Wallflower Designs, Susan McKelvey, 1573 Millersville Road, Millersville, MD 21108. "Remembrances": Victorian signature cartouches (on fabric) for signing Album Blocks, quilt labels, *Scrolls and Banners* (a booklet of nineteenth-century signature banners for tracing onto quilt blocks), pens for inking, etc.

Appendix II: Course Descriptions

The following descriptions of possible quilting classes use *Baltimore Beauties and Beyond* as a textbook. Anyone who would like to teach these course formats or who would like to use these descriptions and materials lists has the author's and the publisher's permission to do so. Appropriate author/book credit would be appreciated. The book's copyright notice, however, prohibits photocopying or other printing of any other material herein, including patterns.

I. A HALF-DAY OR EVENING (THREE-HOUR) COURSE:

"Baltimore Album Quilt Basics." A charming reproduction block teaches you inlaid and onlaid appliqué, perfect points and corners, and the easy art of invisible appliqué. This class introduces you to the delights of making a Baltimore Album Quilt on your own, using *Baltimore Beauties and Beyond, Volume I,* as a step-by-step workbook and guide. You will begin the whole-cloth appliqué block, "Double Hearts" (Pattern #2).

Materials: One 16" square each of off-white background fabric and a medium-size red print, matching red thread, #11 Sharps (appliqué needles), small cut-to-the point scissors for fabric and paper, 12 1/2" square of freezer paper, pencil, dark fabric marker, small straight pins.

II. AN ALL-DAY (FIVE- TO SIX-HOUR) COURSE:

"Two Baltimore Beauty Blocks." This intensive introduction to Baltimore Album Quilt techniques takes you from a one-color block to multicolors, using inlaid and onlaid cutwork appliqué and needleturn with the "freezer paper on top" method.* You'll perfect your technique on points and stitches and progress to more wonderful blocks using *Baltimore Beauties and Beyond, Volume I,* as your guide. You will begin the blocks "Fleur-de-Lis I" (Pattern #1) and "$200,000 Tulips" (Pattern #8). (*Note to teacher: Use the "freezer paper on top" method for the red tulips and the circle of hearts in Pattern #8.)

Materials: Two 16" squares off-white fabric, one 16" square of medium-size red print plus roughly a "fat quarter" of red fabric (small print or plain), one 16" square of green, thread to match colored fabrics, two 12 1/2" squares of freezer paper, #11 Sharps (appliqué needles), small cut-to-the point scissors for fabric and paper, pencil, dark fabric marker, small straight pins.

III. A ONE-YEAR COURSE (TWELVE THREE-HOUR CLASSES):

"A Block-a-Month Baltimore-style Album Quilt." Learn as you go, progressing from the simplest graphic blocks to three-dimensional "fancy flowers." Each block is a classic Album Quilt appliqué lesson from *Baltimore Beauties and Beyond, Volume I.* Making these twelve blocks will instruct, delight, and hasten the completion of your heirloom Album Quilt. A set model for your quilt might be twelve blocks with a medallion center such as "The Fascinating Ladies of Bygone Baltimore," quilt #7, in *Baltimore Beauties, Volume I.*

Note to teachers: This course can lead the way for two more classes based on *Volume II and III.* The first might be "Medallion Centers, Sets, Borders, and Quilting Designs for Your Classic-style Appliqué Album Quilt." A second possible class might be "A Block-a-Month through *Baltimore Beauties and Beyond, Volumes II and III.*" Make an additional 12 blocks towards the classic 25-block set, including the style of blocks that graphically records the evidence of particular lives and times: Scenery Blocks and Portrait Blocks. Such an extended course could also present more advanced techniques through such fascinating Album Quilt block types as Fruits from Mary Evans' Garden and More Fancy Flowers.

IV. CUSTOMIZING YOUR OWN COURSES BASED ON *BALTIMORE BEAUTIES:*

If you choose to teach the lessons in *Baltimore Beauties and Beyond, Volume I,* as separate classes, Lessons 1 through 5 would be three-hour classes, Lessons 6 through 12 would be five- to six-hour classes.

Note to quilt shop owners or guild program chairmen: You might be interested in my coming to your area as a kick-off activity to start on-going local classes with a burst of enthusiasm. I give a one-day overview class and an introductory slide-lecture on the background (historic, symbolic, artistic) of the classic Baltimore Album Quilts. I'd be happy to send my teaching overview letter for your consideration. A stamped, self-addressed envelope would be appreciated. Please write on official letterhead or include other identification with your request to: Elly Sienkiewicz, 5540 30th Street N.W., Washington, D.C. 20015.

THE *BALTIMORE BEAUTIES*® SERIES BY ELLY SIENKIEWICZ:

With the exception of her first, self-published book, all of the author's books are available from C&T Publishing, P.O. Box 1456, Lafayette, California, 94549. (1-800-284-1114)

Spoken Without A Word—A Lexicon of Selected Symbols, With 24 Patterns from Classic Baltimore Album Quilts (1983).
This was the first book to faithfully reproduce patterns from classic Baltimore Album Quilts and to point out the intentional symbolism within these quilts' design motifs. (Available from Vermont Patchworks, Box 229, Shrewsbury, VT 05738. 1-800-451-4044)

Baltimore Beauties and Beyond, Studies in Classic Album Quilt Appliqué, Volume I (1989)
Twelve lessons take the beginner from the simplest Baltimore Album Quilt blocks to the most complex. A wealth of appliqué techniques is presented and 24 Album block patterns are given. Already a classic, this book introduces you to Baltimore-style Album making.

Baltimore Album Quilts, Historic Notes and Antique Patterns, A Pattern Companion to Baltimore Beauties and Beyond, Volume I (1990)
A magnificent 56 patterns offers the framework for sharing Baltimore's fascinating historical saga and close-up pictures of antique blocks and Albums.

Baltimore Beauties and Beyond, Studies in Classic Album Quilt Appliqué, Volume II (1991)
This volume pictures more than 50 antebellum Albums and offers 20 block and 13 border patterns. It teaches the design and making of Picture Blocks and instructs on how to write on your quilts in permanent ink, including the transfer of engraved motifs by ironed-on photocopies.

Appliqué 12 Easy Ways! Charming Quilts, Giftable Projects, and Timeless Techniques (1991)
A very basic how-to-appliqué book illustrated with wonderful clarity. Complete patterns include 29 beautiful projects from gifts to graphic museum replica quilts. Their common thread? All are terrifically appealing and so easy to make! Written for the novice, this book has proven equally popular among experienced appliquérs wishing to learn Elly's "latest pointers" on appliqué.

Dimensional Appliqué—A Pattern Companion to Volume II of Baltimore Beauties and Beyond, Studies in Classic Album Quilt Appliqué (1993)
A best-seller! Simple, innovative methods for dimensional flowers and unique appliqué basketry. All are taught through step-by-step teach-yourself lessons, dozens of block patterns and five border patterns. Whether for stylish accessories or an heirloom quilt, with this book, exquisite flowers bloom at your fingertips!

Appliqué 12 Borders and Medallions! A Pattern Companion to Volume III of Baltimore Beauties and Beyond, Studies in Classic Album Quilt Appliqué (1994)
Here are a dozen patterns—fully drafted and pictured in fabric—for some of the most beautiful fruit and floral borders in the classic Albums. Two magnificent —and easy—enlarged central medallion patterns are included: one from Baltimore, one from "beyond."

About the Author

Papercuts and Plenty—Volume III of Baltimore Beauties and Beyond, Studies in Classic Album Quilt Appliqué (1995) Papercut Appliqué Albums have always been the author's favorite stylistic stream in the antebellum Baltimores. *Volume III* offers an in-depth study of how to make Albums in this surprisingly expressive style. Included in this volume is a fascinating historical analysis of what caused the Baltimore Albums to bloom so profusely, who made these famous quilts, why the style spread so widely, and what brought the Album era to an end?

For a complete list of other fine quilting books from C&T Publishing, Inc., write for a free catalog:
C&T PUBLISHING, INC.
P.O. BOX 1456 • LAFAYETTE, CA 94549
1(800)284-1114
http://www.ctpub.com

Elly Sienkiewicz's fascination with the Baltimore Album Quilts combines old loves—history, religion, and art—and is now of many years' duration. In 1983, Elly self-published *Spoken Without a Word: A Lexicon of Selected Symbols with 24 Patterns from Classic Baltimore Album Quilts*. Winners of a contest based on that book became latter-day "Ladies of Baltimore." The group has since grown. Through their help, Elly has produced several Appliqué Album Quilts shown in these volumes. She draws upon over two dozen years of teaching experience in writing *Baltimore Beauties and Beyond*.

She holds degrees in history and education from Wellesley College and the University of Pennsylvania. Before specializing in quilts and quiltmaking, Elly taught secondary school for seven years. The silhouette self-portrait in pen and ink is from a photo by Elly's husband, Stan Sienkiewicz.

ABOUT THE BACK COVER

Yearning to Breathe Free, block B-1 in quilt #7 (Pattern #23). Designed and appliquéd by Elly Sienkiewicz; quilting designed and quilted by Hazel B. Reed Ferrell.

Block design based on a block of the Washington Monument in Baltimore from a circa 1852 quilt for Miss Isabella Battee, now in the collection of the Baltimore Museum of Art. Pattern #23 for this contemporary version includes a married couple, to suggest other possible centers for this Lyre Wreath design. A pattern for the classic original block appears in the author's previous book, *Spoken Without a Word*.

Many public buildings and monuments were depicted in the classic Baltimore Quilts and the Washington Monument (shown in Photo 5) was a particular favorite. In Elly's version, the Statue of Liberty appears because it has become as significant to twentieth-century Americans as monuments to George Washington were to nineteenth-century Americans.